CENTRE

OTHER PUBLICATIONS

Worm's Eye View
Blindness Kindness
Going Out There is No Other
Coming Back There is No Trace
Blondin: Collected Poems
Bamboo Leaves
Oxford Blues
Gnomonic Verses
Vienna
Vajras & Dorjes
Basic Buddhism for a World in Trouble
What is Buddhism?
The Living Waters of Buddhism
Buddhism and Drugs
Basic Buddhist Meditation
The Five Buddhist Precepts
Dependent Origination *(Paṭiccasamuppāda)*
The Ten Fetters *(Saŋyojana)*
The Five Hindrances *(Nivāranas)*
Buddhist Pali Chants with English Translations
The Universal Octopus & Mr Tao
Previous Lives & Astrals

CENTRE

The Truth about Everything

BRIAN TAYLOR

www.universaloctopus.com

Published by Universal Octopus 2016
www.universaloctopus.com

COPYRIGHT © 2009-2011 BRIAN F TAYLOR

A catalogue record of this book is available from the British Library.

ISBN 978-0-9571901-6-0

All rights reserved. No part of this publication may be used or reproduced in any manner without the prior written permission of the copyright owner, except for 'fair use' as brief quotations embodied in articles and reviews.

CONTENTS

PROLOGUE 5

NOTES ON TERMINOLOGY 9

PART ONE
A SHORT HISTORY OF THE UNIVERSE

1. IN THE BEGINNING 15
2. A LITTLE LATER 16
3. I AM ! 17
4. AWAKENING 18
5. ANOTHER ? 19
6. FRIENDLINESS 20
7. SUSPICION & HOSTILITY 21
8. THE UNIVERSAL OCTOPUS 22
9. INCARNATION 26
10. DEVELOPMENT IN THE WOMB 29
11. BIRTH 32
12. THE STAIRCASE TO OTHER WORLDS 34

PART TWO
THE CENTRE

13. THE CREATION AND COLONISATION OF MATTER 43
14. GETTING STARTED 49
15. LOCATING THE CENTRE 51
16. EXPLORATION 56
17. THE CENTRE AS SOURCE 66

18. HEALING 77
19. HEALING OTHERS 82
20. HOSTILITY AND FEAR 84
21. HOSTILITY FROM OTHERS 86
22. UPSTREAMING 87

PART THREE
HOW EVERYTHING WORKS AND WHAT IT CAN ACHIEVE

23. CHAKRAS 97
24. EXPLORING OTHER CENTRES 110
25. CHART A 133
26. CHART B 134
27. THE THREE CHANNELS 135
28. ASTRALS AND ASTRAL TRAVEL 137
29. ASTRALS, DEVAS AND BRAHMĀS 143
30. MORE BODIES 153
31. KUNDALINI 161
32. LONGEVITY 171
33. THE PHILOSOPHER'S STONE 173
34. CREATIVITY AND THE CENTRE 176
35. OTHER METHODS 182
36. REMEMBERING PAST LIVES 183
37. BLOWING THE FUSE 190

    EPILOGUE 193

PROLOGUE

I discovered the Centre one night on a bridge over the River Chao Phya. I was thirty.

I was thinking about Prince Siddhartha. At twenty-nine, the Prince, going out from his palace, had seen an old man, a sick man, a dead man and a wandering ascetic.

He realised that sickness, old age and death happened to men whether they had palaces or not. He came to the conclusion that,

"This world has fallen on hard times."

He left his family and home to seek the Truth.

Six years later, he had become the Buddha and proclaimed that the solution to the problem of suffering lay in *giving up this world* and all attachment to it.*

During the Buddha's lifetime, some monks, on attaining the stage of Arahant (the final stage of perfection), did not wait for their lives to come to a natural end, but "took the knife". That is, they killed themselves. This really did seem an uncompromising way of "giving up the world".

The Buddha did not condemn them for this. He said it was a decision they were entitled to take and did not in any way affect their level of attainment. He did, however, discourage other monks from doing it, as it was getting the

---

* *and any other world.*

Order of Monks undesirable publicity among those who did not understand.

I walked across the river on one side of the bridge and back again on the other side. Several times. I stopped in the middle and looked down at the muddy water. It seemed that if life was in fact undesirable and the very source of suffering, and that death at some time was in any case inevitable, then it was perfectly reasonable to put an end to it sooner rather than later. I could find no attraction or attachment in myself at that moment for anything in the world. My hand rested on the handrail.

I realised that, for all its reasonableness, it was nevertheless a jump in the dark. Unlike the Buddha and his Arahants, I had not already discovered where I would be heading.

Furthermore, if they had discovered something "beyond the world", how had they discovered it while still "in the world"?

I continued to walk to and fro across the bridge. I noted the odd fact that, although it was not particularly late and it carried a main road out of Bangkok, no traffic or pedestrians had appeared on it since I arrived.

I resumed my train of thought. How do you find out what lies beyond the world before actually leaving it? This did not seem to be something that thinking could resolve.

At this point, various names given to the Buddha began to arise spontaneously in my mind as a kind of list. The Perfect One, the Fully Enlightened One, the All Knowing One, the Blissful One, the Blessed One... What caught my attention was the repetition of the word "One".

Of course these titles are English translations. The original Pali does not have (nor need) an equivalent of our "one". Nevertheless, the titles continued to present themselves in this way and I found myself quietly murmuring: -

One and not two,
That's all you have to do.
One and not two,
That's all you have to do.

My thinking petered out and came to an end. But I did not jump.

To my surprise, a feeling of good humour *arose*. Where from? It came from deep in the centre of my stomach where something, unexpectedly, became bright and smiled.

I didn't quite feel as though I had found something. I didn't quite feel that something had found me. I felt a sense of boundless integration.

I saw that the whole world, together with the senses that contacted the world, were, and had always been, *outside* and were and had always been the source of every conceivable form of suffering and inconvenience.

Later I came to see that all beings had this luminous Centre at the centre of their being and were, for the most part, unaware of its significance or even its existence.

This book contains the results of some of my researches into the Centre. Some may find it interesting.

However, in these matters as in others, the only experience that is of any use to you is your own. People can eulogise a particular brand of tea, but until you have tasted it yourself, it is second-hand experience. It may even be coffee.

When the buffalo comes to the edge of the enclosure,
horns, head and body pass through the bars quite easily.
But not the tail!

NOTES ON TERMINOLOGY

I have used the term **CENTRE** because it exactly expresses the meaning and the location.

When a *particular* centre is named, I have used "**chakra**", e.g. *Heart Chakra, Brain Chakra* etc. The Sanskrit word is familiar and is mostly used by those who have studied this subject.

This also avoids confusion with the "Centre" which is quite different from the "centres" (chakras). The Centre is upstream of the chakras. The chakras (and everything else) derive from it.

However, I have not used the Indian names for the chakras. Writers do not all use the same labels. They differ as to what they think the functions of chakras are. They sometimes disagree as to where they are located.

Mostly, I have preferred English words which describe their location and/or function e.g. *Base Chakra, Desire Chakra*.

An exception to this is *Brahmā Chakra*. This chakra is outside the body, a few inches above the aperture of brahma. It is inaccessible to Kundalini and links to the highest heavens of form. When it is entered, the form perceived is often the Great Brahmā with four faces indicating "all-seeing" and four (or more) arms indicating "all-doing", or a similar, exalted "Creator" being. (See page 122). I have also referred to the *Brahmā Channel*.

When referring to the subsidiary centres in general, these are sometimes referred to as "centres", sometimes "chakras".

I have used the name "**Kundalini**" for the primary source of that form of energy which appears as desire and is imbedded in matter. The name is well known. It comes from Sanskrit and means "coiled" or "the coiled one". In actual experience, when it is located in the Base Chakra, it always has the form of a snake.

I have used the Sanskrit "**karma**" rather than the Pali "kamma". But I have used the Pali "**Nibbāna**" in preference to the Sanskrit "Nirvāna". I can see no justification for this.

I have used "**birth**" and "**rebirth**" rather than "incarnation" and "reincarnation".

"Incarnation" suggests a permanent self, entering into matter. "Reincarnation" suggests that it has left one material form and entered another. In each case the self is assumed to be basically an unchanging entity.

This sounds similar to someone getting in and out of cars. It is commonly assumed that it is the same, enduring person who gets out of one car and gets into another. One could hardly expect to persuade a policeman that the man he saw getting out of the Ford (oneself) was not the man who immediately got into, and is now sitting in, the Rover (oneself).

Not even if one quoted the poet T.S.Eliot,

> "*You are not the same people who left that station*
> *Or who will arrive at any terminus.......*"

One would find difficulty in getting the traffic policeman to agree with Mr. Eliot. In this case, the poet is closer to the

Truth than the English traffic policeman (which may surprise you). If there really were an unchanging fixed self which transmigrated from body to body eternally, that self would not escape from suffering; from endlessly being born and dying.

There are those who take this view, however, and, if they see the long-term implications, it is a bleak prospect.

The truth is somewhat different (as one discovers by using the Centre). What seems to be the individual is a *continuum* and not an entity that continues indefinitely. At any moment it is not the same as at any point in the past, but it is not different either.

Another poet, Tennyson, described the continuum as "rising on stepping stones of our dead selves to higher things". He neglected to mention that there are others "descending on stepping stones of their dead selves to lower things". There is both an ascent into light and a descent into darkness.

"Birth" and "rebirth" can be explained in a way that clarifies the matter. A candle burns because of the fuel in it (karma). It will go out when the fuel is exhausted. If, as it goes out, its flame ignites the supply of fuel which forms another candle (unresolved karma), the fire will continue to burn.

There is continuity from candle to candle but one could never say that the *candle* has reincarnated. What passes over from candle to candle (the flame) is desire. The consequence is fresh entanglement in the endless flow of karma (new candle). If desire comes to an end, that is the end of the sequence of burning candles; no matter how many there have been. Without the flame, the wax (old karma) is inoperative.

Those who see the undesirability of endless candles (birth-death-rebirth) seek a way of putting out the flame of desire.

Those who delight in becoming, who seek out births and put up as best they can with the inevitable deaths, put fuel on the flame of their desire by feeding it with selective images and memories – the good times.

I have retained "**incarnation**" only twice. In chapter 9, which deals with the non-material Centre incarnating into matter as it creates the Many out of the One; and on page 48, in the image of the sheaths.

I have used the word "**universe**" because it comes from "unus", *one* and "vertere" to *rotate* or *change*. This gives the idea of something, which is a unity, rotating and rolling on, ever changing. Because it is One, it is everything that exists, has existed and will exist; and also everything that might exist or does not exist.

Within this context, I have drawn a distinction between **mind** and **matter** on the basis that matter is composed of atomic and subatomic particles and that mind is not. It follows that the mental planes of being - heaven worlds, astral plane etc. - do not have the same restrictions as the material world.

Mental objects or events cannot, therefore, be perceived by sense organs and instruments whose function is to perceive material phenomena. The mental worlds do, in fact, have restrictions but they are not the same as the restrictions that apply to matter. They can be perceived by mind-made sense organs.

PART ONE

A SHORT HISTORY OF THE UNIVERSE

One and not two,
That's all you have to do.
One and not two,
That's all you have to do.

1. IN THE BEGINNING

HOW IT WAS IN THE BEGINNING,
IS NOW
AND EVER WILL BE.

COMPLETE PERFECT PEACE.
THIS IS THE BEGINNING,
THE BEGINNINGLESS BEGINNING,
THE CENTRE AND CIRCUMFERENCE
OF ALL LIVING BEINGS IN ALL UNIVERSES,
EVERYWHERE, ALWAYS, WITHOUT END.

2. A LITTLE LATER

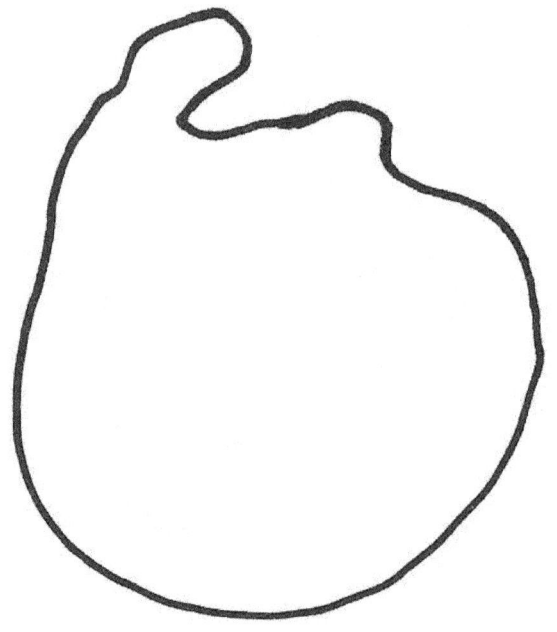

*THE STIRRING OF AN OUTWARD AWARENESS,
A BARELY PERCEPTIBLE CURIOSITY.*

3. I AM !......

........WHAT I AM !

4. AWAKENING

*A SURPRISE. THE UNEXPECTED SEEING
OF ONE'S FACE IN A MIRROR
BEFORE THERE ARE ANY MIRRORS!
HALF RECOGNITION, HALF DOUBT.*

5. ANOTHER?

ONE CREATES THE *APPEARANCE* OF ANOTHER.

6. FRIENDLINESS

YOU *AND* ME

COMPASSION

LOVE

SYMPATHETIC JOY

RECOGNITION OF SAMENESS/DIFFERENCE

HAPPINESS

TOGETHERNESS.

7. SUSPICION & HOSTILITY

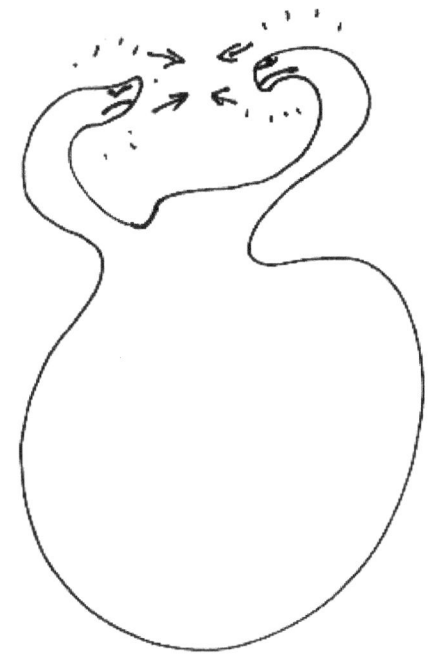

YOU *OR* ME

THE RIVALS
THE COMPETITION, THE ENEMY,
FEAR, ENVY, DISTRUST, SUSPICION, DISLIKE,
ANGER, HATE.

8. THE UNIVERSAL OCTOPUS

Each tentacle that used to be anonymous
Is now by mutual consent autonomous.
At first they may behave a bit like fools
But they'll do better when they know the rules.

As the tentacles reach out they take on material form. They are manifestations of the Centre and therefore not identical to it. But not separate from it either.

A whole world of beings! Friends and enemies. Allies and foes. Mine and theirs. All struggling with each other to survive. Competing with each other for the same goals, the same territory, the same possessions.

"Alone and afraid in a world I never made."

The Centre is the centre and circumference of everything.

The tentacles reach out from it and subside back into it. Like waves in the ocean. The energy that keeps this going is Desire. Desire to experience Other. There is no Other. Only other appearances of the same thing. The Centre. If a tentacle strikes a tentacle, it is not striking another. It is striking the One. It is striking itself. This is why karma works as it does.

What you do to another, you do to you.

It is done to you by you.

The tentacles look *out* at each other. The outward-looking senses make it appear that that tentacle is over *there*. Whereas I am *here*.

The computer/brain immediately calculates and comes up with: based on the evidence, since these two things are not connected, they are separate. That's *you*. This is *me*.

The computer is not malfunctioning.

Based on the evidence presented to it, its conclusion is valid.

With the diagram we can see that the tentacles are all joined at the base and in no way separated from the content of the Centre. But the tentacles are the product of an outward-looking sense represented by their eyes. Their eyes can only see tentacles.

To see where they are joined together needs another sense that is not outward-looking. The tentacles, you, me and the others, are not really joined at the feet. We would soon see it if they were. We are joined at the Centre. The Centre is not outside the tentacle, not outside our bodies. It is *inside.* Right at the centre of our bodies. Right at the centre of the tentacle, which in the diagram is represented by its base, beyond which it just merges into the undifferentiated One.

The tentacles can reach out as far as they like and develop as many eyes (or other senses) as they wish. They only ever see more and more tentacles.

If they want to find the origin of everything, including tentacles, they have to look back inside, withdraw back inside and travel back inside. So it is with you and me.

"Riding backwards on an ox, I enter the Buddha Hall."

9. INCARNATION

Incarnation, conception, begins when there is an impulse and movement away and out. Outward seeking gives rise to a sense organ, which sees something outside. It doesn't see anything outside *itself.* That is not possible. It sees something outside its *form.* The form is the outside of the invisible gateway at the base of the tentacle. Inside the gate is the undifferentiated oneness, which is the source of

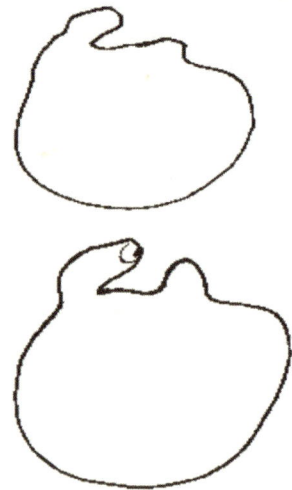

everything and from which absolutely anything can (and does) arise.

In human beings, this gateway, the Centre, occupies a physical location. But only just. In the centre of the body behind the navel, in front of the spine. Two inches above the solar plexus.

In the womb, you start as a fertilised egg. The fertilised egg forms around this gateway. When you are conceived, the fertilised egg is a physical thing but it is also the gateway between the non-material that you are and come from and the material existence (the egg) into which you are reaching out to be born.

The egg is a minute particle of matter. In its centre is an entry point to non-matter. The egg can be examined by physical instruments. The entry point cannot be. Because it is not matter. The source appears in the egg as livingness. If this entry point is absent, as for example in an unfertilised egg, because the egg is just matter, it disintegrates and disappears.

The non-physical side of the gateway is non-matter, the source of all things that come into existence and into which they subside again when the living impulse runs out of energy.

Through this gateway, you are born; into it you die. Into it you fall, when you *fall* asleep. You bring no thing with you when you come in. You take no thing with you when you go out. When you die, if there is still an impulse to become something separate, you reappear through a gateway into another form, another tentacle.

Precisely what form you take on depends upon your karma, that is, what you have been up to in your previous appearances, your previous lives.

The Centre is not only the way *into* this world from the non material it is also the entry *from* this world into all other worlds, other planes of reality. (See chapter 12). It is possible to access these, while you are still alive, as a "tourist" as it were, if you can master the art of *consciously* exiting through the gateway and sustaining

27

this consciousness on the other side. (See chapter 16).

Of course, you enter the Centre in deep sleep. But, since there is no awareness, there is no memory either, because there is no thing to remember. Dreams occur before and after deep sleep and usually relate to activities in the brain centre, which is why an electroencephalograph (EEG) can register them. But the EEG cannot register the Centre because there is no thing to register.

10. DEVELOPMENT IN THE WOMB

The egg develops materially by absorbing the food stream that flows into it from the mother through the umbilical cord, which is located near the gate between matter and non-matter. The material being goes through changes of form before it begins to look like the small human, which will eventually emerge, still attached to its nutrient line, at birth.

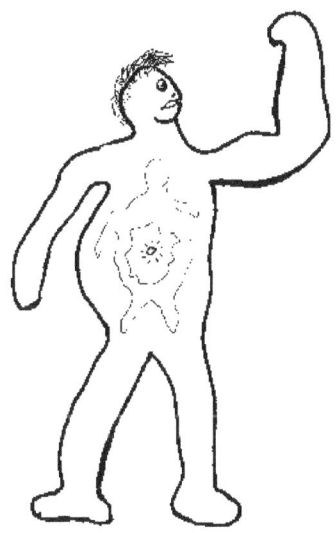

The physical link with your mother, the umbilical cord, provides physical food that allows physical growth. The expanding and elongating physical form also comes with more refined non-physical expansion into matter.

During development in the womb the Centre remains unchanged. It is still the gateway between the born and the unborn. It never ceases to be a doorway between the born and the unborn. Its physical side can be contacted by material instruments, the non-physical side by mental instruments.

As the embryo grows, the Centre pushes energy out, upwards and downwards, giving rise to subsidiary centres inside the material body. These subsidiary centres can be called "chakras". The most important of these above the Centre for humans are, in order of appearance, the one in the centre of the chest (called the Heart Chakra) and the one in the centre of the head (the Brain Chakra).

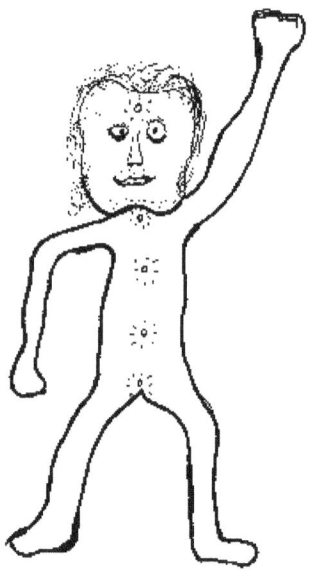

The one in the head is of great importance because it is around this that the physical brain develops. This is a computer and it is in the brain that the experiences of this life are stored and can be accessed as thoughts and mental images. It is what goes on in the brain that a man normally associates with himself. *I think, I remember etc.*

The energy from the Centre also pushes downwards and creates secondary centres lower in the developing body. The two most important of these are the Solar Plexus Chakra and the Base Chakra. (See chapters 23, 25). The Desire Chakra is also important because of its function in the physical procreation of the species.

11. BIRTH

When you have completed your period of growth in the womb, your mother's body pushes you out. If you are receiving conventional medical assistance, someone cuts the umbilical cord and you are ready (or unready) to go it alone.

Alone is how it seems. Because all your physical sense organs face outwards, the brain quickly comes to the conclusion that you are separate from what you perceive. Awareness of the Centre remains at first and, in many cases, the information bombarding you from the outside is balanced by an awareness of where you came from through the gateway.

This awareness is to some extent stored in the brain too. But because of all the information coming in from outside and the efforts of the human beings around you to attract your attention and exteriorise it, this awareness gradually fades. When you sleep, you go straight back into the Centre and this helps to balance many of the difficult experiences of the very young baby and keeps you sane.

Nowadays, in the "Developed" world, it is unusual for anyone to sustain clear recall of the other side of the gateway and the previous births and experiences which can be accessed by going back through it. Therefore, it is quite soon that you accept that you are an independent, separate being in a here and now, even though there may still linger on memories that you were once something else and somewhere else. Before.

But, as you grow up and away, the non-material Centre

remains the same and invisible to the outward-looking sense organs. It, or rather the energy which continues to come out from it into the body, can be felt in the region of the solar plexus. Especially if you put your hand upon your stomach to cover the area above the navel.

It is through the Centre that you came in. It is through this same Centre that you will leave, to reappear in other worlds and on other planes of reality. These you will have to leave too. You carry on transmigrating, wandering on and on endlessly, until you find a way out. A way to bring about an end to this process of becoming and ceasing, getting born and dying.

Discovering the Centre is the first step towards bringing this process to an end.

It is similar to a prisoner discovering which of all the hundreds of doors in the prison is the exit door. He still has to find a key and open it.

But he has made a start.

12. THE STAIRCASE TO OTHER WORLDS

Imagine a block of apartments with a central staircase. The staircase links all the different floors and on each floor there are doors into the apartments on that floor. But behind these doors are not apartments, but complete levels of being, complete worlds.

Each level is a complete world with:
a birth (in through the door)
a death (out through the door)
and, in between, *a life* in that world.

Going through a door means being born into that world. Coming back out again is dying. All the various activities of life go on behind the door. The growing up. The learning. The relationships. The acquisition of possessions, the pleasures and pains, the joys and sorrows. The attachments. When you die, you have to leave it all behind. Everything you have acquired. *Even your body.* Because it is dead.

Some worlds have more than one door. Our world for example. Ours is a complex world with many levels of reality and levels of being.

There is a door for human beings. Humans are, currently, the dominant living beings and act in a way that affects all the others. But many of the other living beings, earthworms, insects, bacteria, the vegetative world, have no particular awareness of us. We are just part of the background of "otherness".

They have their own doors. There is a door for beings like fish and crabs. The door opens into the same world, but underwater. There is a door for insects. There is a door for animals.

It is not uncommon for a human being to leave this world by the door he came in (the human door) and come back in again by a different door. It is possible for farmers to return as calves; fishermen to come back as fish.

> *The fisherman sees the fish*
> *but not its pain*
> *until as fish*
> *he swims this way again.*
>
> *(Blondin)*

This is because of the underlying oneness of everything (see Universal Octopus picture). If a fisherman can't understand that he is causing suffering to the fish, then he will have to come back as a fish to experience the suffering he has caused. He may have premonitions of this. He starts to have dreams that develop into nightmares in which he is in the sea struggling in nets or swimming under bridges from which fishing lines are hanging before his nose. If these dreams don't encourage him to reassess what he is doing or has done, then re-entry as a fish is almost certain.

> *He who kills the fly*
> *must feel the spider's wrath.*
>
> *(William Blake)*

This is something that can be verified by someone who learns how to visit these worlds, temporarily, while still alive, as a "tourist".

Acting as a tourist, it is possible to go out of the door of this world onto the staircase (leaving the body behind) and visit some of the other worlds to verify these things and gain knowledge about the way karma works and the lessons that can be learned when one returns to one's own life.

The fisherman's dreams are a version of this. It differs from "tourism" in two ways. Firstly, it is involuntary. The fisherman doesn't choose these dreams. Secondly he is not an observer but a participant. He experiences a fish's plight as a fish. Entomologists have similar dreams involving spiders and their webs. Dairy and poultry farmers do too.

The Staircase extends above the floor on which we are currently living as human beings in this world and also below.

The highest floor has a door that opens into no world at all but an indescribable state that lies behind all the other worlds. This is similar to the way a cinema screen is always behind whatever films are projected onto it. It is never in any way affected by the content of the films and their images. Raging fires do not burn it. Seascapes do not make it wet.

This is Nibbāna. You can't exactly call it a level because it has no boundaries and lies behind all phenomena just as the screen is found behind all films and their images. But it is reached, in this method, by ascending through a series of higher and more refined levels, which lead to the gateway to it.

Briefly, by using the staircase, one finds that as the levels get higher, they are progressively finer and subtler and the beings that inhabit them are finer and happier too. It is possible to communicate just as a tourist does, by asking the locals he meets in his travels questions that come to his mind. Language, however, is not a factor.

The only time one doesn't get an answer is when the question cannot be answered on that level. Beings cannot provide answers about things that are beyond their comprehension. Just as a driver can tell you about driving but may not be able to explain how a car works.

The lower levels are progressively coarser and unhappier. Their inhabitants correspond to this. The potential for misery is unimaginable and not everyone can bring himself to witness it.

What does become clear, both while one is experiencing these things and later when one reflects on it all, is that everything proceeds by cause and effect. Vast networks of interrelated causes and their interacting consequences. One is left with no doubt about this and no longer puts anything down to chance. Despite the complexity of it all, it becomes quite clear that, as far as an individual is concerned, the answer to it all is very simple indeed: do good, get good; do bad, get bad.

What is good and bad? Good is being helpful and not doing anything to others that one doesn't like being done to oneself. Bad is the opposite of this. Everything done is done to the Centre and the consequences reflect back.

Everywhere we go we come to the same conclusion. We also realise that so long as we are aware of this, we are in a position to take charge of our own destinies without needing to rely on others.

Advanced: If we understand, we can press the cause buttons that produce the effects we want.

Further exploration and understanding reveal that all levels have a basic pattern. We enter, we leave. We can stay in the Highest Heavens for a long time. We cannot stay forever. Our time runs out.

Very Advanced: We come to realise intuitively, or experience directly, that there *is* a permanent state, which is Perfect Peace. But to enter it, you can't take anything with you. Not even your own identity and separateness. Not even your own shadow.

Intuitively, we *realise* that by giving up even the desire for a sense of separateness, we can enter:

and recognise it (and ourselves) for the first time.

It can be directly *experienced*, too, but this is rare. To do so, we leave, in succession, all the other levels and, reaching a moment at which one finds every aspect of mental and physical existence to be unsatisfactory, one's understanding mirrors this. When this happens, when experience and understanding balance perfectly, desire evaporates. Because nothing is seen as desirable. Even the impulse towards separate identity loses its energy (desire):

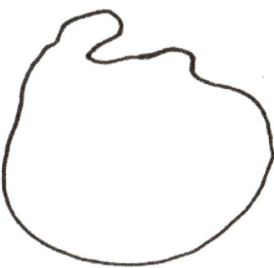

and one experiences the unconditioned state.

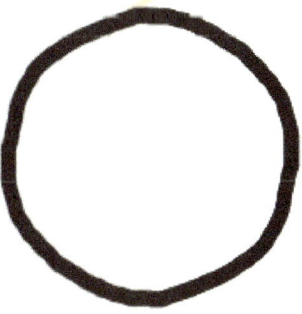

Temporarily. It is totally unexpected and indescribable.

Later, one returns to one's normal physical awareness in the current lifetime in this world. One can review one's experience and measure it against the constant flow of material and mental sense objects that make up life. One can see any remaining mental fetters that bind one to this level of existence. One investigates these and the objects of these desires. One sees how all objects of desire are the same. They have a beginning and an end. Just like life itself; there is a birth and a death. One turns away from them.

On turning away, we reach the end of the cycle of transmigration through this universe with its myriad apparently separate things. Forever.

It is technically possible to decide to postpone our final entry into Nibbāna (that is continue to be reborn) in order to help others find a way out. Many try. It is usually not successful. The wandering spirit's keenness of understanding dulls under the bombardment of sense impressions and it becomes caught again in the net of becoming. It continues to be subject to former karma and, in ignorance, creates more new karma.

Gradually, then with increasing velocity, it sinks down into lower realms. And forgets.

PART TWO

THE CENTRE

The fisherman sees the fish
  but not its pain
  until as fish
he swims this way again.

13. THE CREATION AND COLONISATION OF MATTER

Note: This is a historical description. Why is it not in the past tense? Because it is also continually happening in the present. It will continue to do so until, and unless, the sangsāra is emptied.

There is the original Centre.

As the outward push from the Centre into the creation and perception of mind and matter develops (see chapter 8), subsidiary centres appear, each energising a specific area of the mental or physical body. For us, most of the main ones appear in a straight line, vertically, in the middle of the physical body.

This process is a colonisation of mind and matter* and these subsidiary centres form outposts of the Centre. The Centre is continually creating a more solidified version of itself, together with sense organs capable of perceiving its creation and thus satisfying a nascent curiosity (see chapter 2).

Initially, it is *wholly* mental and contains none of the atomic and subatomic building blocks which we associate with the physical universe and which we perceive with our physical senses.

---

* Strictly speaking, each higher level (higher = nearer the Centre) creates the level below it by intention. So the mind "colonises matter" <u>as it creates it!</u>

Duality and pluralism have come into existence (see chapter 3). The colonisation and organisation of apparently independent mental beings is being brought about by these subsidiary centres (chakras).

The chakras on the mental plane also act as the sense-organs of the mental beings. They increase in number during devolution and, by the time the level of mental expansion has reached the deva/astral planes, the colonisation is ready to solidify further.

This is the plane of what we perceive as material existence. When human beings appear on this level, their bodies normally contain the chakras as they appear in Chart A. (See page 133.)

These chakras, which are the sense-organs of mental bodies, are reaching out into the denser matter which is forming and creating physical duplicates of themselves (see chapter 28). They also channel energy from the Centre into our five senses in a form which they need to continue to function.

This means that if the astral form, with its astral senses, withdraws for a sufficient length of time from the physical, our five senses will cease to function. That is, physically, we die.

The physical plane of being, the material universe, contains all those beings and organisms which have physical bodies. They can be contacted using physical senses. They can also be investigated with physical, scientific instruments.

The transition from the deva/astral to the physical is achieved as the chakras attract to themselves the atomic and subatomic matter which is concurrently coming into existence. It is similar to the way a magnet attracts iron filings and thereby makes its magnetic field visible to the human, physical eye.

The physical form of the human approximates to the deva form of which it is a crude copy. Using the outward movement from the Centre and the mental stream of energy which emanates from it, the chakras create the physical form. Each chakra organises the physical organs which come into existence in the matter which surrounds it. They are also instrumental in the creation of the sense organs which enable the physical universe to be perceived and explored. These sense organs are material facsimiles of the mental sense organs which pre-exist on the deva planes of existence.

These secondary centres are "outposts" of the Centre. The feelings that turbulate in the area around the Centre and elsewhere have their origins in these secondary centres. These feelings are the result of contact made at the sense doors with the material world. In the human form there are five of these sense doors.

The Centre is the source of all energy. Everything in the material universe is emitting this original energy, transmutcd in many ways, into the universe around it. If it didn't, it would not exist or be perceptible in the material universe. Though it might exist and be perceptible elsewhere. Because every "thing" is emitting energy, this energy can be perceived by another "thing" if it has the necessary sense organs to do so.

If the object or event (one or more objects *doing* something) emits an electromagnetic field within the (limited) range that our **eyes** can respond to, we **see** it.

If it propels molecules of air, water or gas within the range our **ears** can respond to, we **hear** it. What causes sound? Vibrations cause sound. An object that vibrates causes the medium around it to compress at a certain frequency. If the frequency is within the range of the ear, it is perceived as sound. The faster things vibrate, the higher the pitch of the sound that is produced. If the pitch is too high for *our* ears, we don't hear it. But the dog might still be able to hear it.

If molecules trigger receptors (a patch of specialised neurons about the size of a postage stamp) in the **nose**, we **smell**.

Taste buds are tiny nerve endings in the **tongue** that allow us to distinguish the different qualities of things we put into our mouth so that we can **taste** them.

Nerve receptors in the outer layer of the **skin** give us the sense of **touch.** This is the first of the five senses to develop in the womb. Through the sense of touch, we can detect texture, temperature, vibration, pressure, heat and cold.

All these perceptions of sense data are fundamentally neutral. More simply, they could be expressed as pressure and temperature. What distinguishes them and particularises them is the interpretation that is put upon them in the brain.

The sense perceptions are not really perceived at the point of contact (eye, ear, nose, tongue and skin), but at the points of discrimination in the brain. It is there also that we come to distinguish them, in a more refined way, as pain and pleasure.

The fundamental *measure* of discrimination (see page 100*ff*) is survival. If something is perceived as pro-survival, we want it. If it appears anti-survival, we reject it. We are not always right about this, but experience is our teacher and memory records the verdict of the learning experience in the brain.

Since we find some things, which are pro-survival, *pleasant* and others that are anti-survival, *unpleasant,* pleasure and pain may become our principal measuring stick. It may not always be infallible. Alcoholics, drug addicts, gamblers and those who are overpowered by strong negative or destructive feelings discover that what seems pleasant (and pro-survival) today, may appear the opposite tomorrow.

It all comes down to the struggle to survive,

the endlessly obstructed urge just to stay alive.

All (including dog) use just one rule as measure;

avoidance of pain and pursuit of pleasure.

Pain leaves an imprint which says, "Leave it be!"

The sirens of pleasure leave a note, "Follow me!"

(Blondin)

This completes the description of how we have come to be what we are, here and now. It also shows the overall route which we have taken from our point of origin.

It is the opposite of modern views which trace the origin of life to an accidental occurrence in matter in the distant past.

It is also different from views that our evolution is ever upwards towards higher levels of being. Supermen, perhaps, or angels or even gods.

We <u>do</u> have the opportunity to make such a journey, but it is towards a goal <u>from which we have previously devolved</u> through a combination of curiosity, ignorance and desire. It is a <u>return</u> journey from a place we have come to see as unsatisfactory, life as we know it, to somewhere completely perfect, the Centre.

Since we have devolved *out of* the Centre, we carry with us, in our continuums, the beings we have been along the way.

This can be compared to a hand reaching out and feeling its way into a glove. The hand cannot be seen but the glove could not move if the hand were not inside. Then it reaches out into another glove and another and another. Always it is the last glove which is in view, on the level in which that glove exists. Always the other gloves, and ultimately the hand itself, are hidden inside it, latent and concealed.

Or you could visualise it as starting off naked. Then getting into a wet suit. Then getting into a diver's suit. Then into a robot. You end up appearing to others (and the mirror) as the last "incarnation", the robot. But the others are still there; like a series of sheaths or Russian dolls.

We still have within us the mental being (the latest glove, the robot) together with the chakras, which are the sense organs of the astral and deva planes. These are mostly latent or semi-conscious in our current, human state.

Although, if they didn't function at all, we could not live and, when they withdraw from our physical bodies altogether, we die. But it is possible to reawaken them and use them on our path back to the Highest Happiness. Why should we delay?

14. GETTING STARTED

One needs to remember that the Centre is *your* centre, the gateway to your real self, where you came in and where you go out, and it is *also* the Centre of the universe. Your Centre and the Centre of the universe are not two things.

If you consider that the Centre and source of the universe has produced everything that exists and has ever existed; microbes, mammoths, mountains, stars, solar systems, black holes, flowers, machines, poetry, music and everything else, you will see the significance of this.

Because everything *was* possible, everything *is* possible.

And the source of this enormous potential power is *inside* you at a precise location, which cannot register on any modern scientific instrument.

So how to begin? Not everyone can. However, at a later stage, you will be able to *see* that all living beings - dogs, cats, insects, humans - have this Centre. (Otherwise they could not exist).

But access for most of them is limited either to sleep or between births.

Conscious access is limited to a few. There's no prohibition. It's just a question of differing levels of development. A worm senses vibrations and feels through touch. But it cannot see, hear and think as we can.

Moreover, it is not *aware* that it doesn't. So it is with beings. They cannot *see* the Centre and they are not aware that they don't.

So a normal man, with all his senses intact, in good health and alert, tends to be mentally imprisoned in thought-patterns, most of which are either the contents of the present life, the existing brain, or earlier versions of this.

He is programmed to survive in the world as he knows it. He is unlikely to have any interest in exploring something of whose existence he is unaware.

Of course we are not entirely without experience of something so fundamental. But we lack conscious, waking experience. Because our usual experience of the Centre is in sleep.

15. LOCATING THE CENTRE

Usually we go there when we sleep. We (our consciousness) sink *down*, which is why we talk about *falling* asleep. Sometimes we can actually feel ourselves falling. We have the same experience when we faint. We feel ourselves falling into the Centre and then, since our consciousness has withdrawn from the brain, our body falls to the ground.

It is similar when we die. The difference is that, at death, there is a withdrawal from the heart as well. So, although we still fall to the ground, the life force has completely withdrawn into the Centre and does not, normally, return. I say "normally" because, rarely, people do come back.

Although we actually enter the Centre in deep sleep, we are unaware of this and when we wake up there is nothing to remember except, "My! I've had a good sleep."

When we are miserable or unhappy, it is to sleep that we want to go. If we find it difficult to sleep, we become disturbed. If this goes on for long, we go and get pills to drive our consciousness out of the brain and down into the Centre. Young children, who are unhappy in their environment, just withdraw into the Centre (fall asleep) at all sorts of odd times. There is even a name for this. Narcolepsy.

What about dreams? When consciousness falls towards the Centre it becomes weak and fitful, flitting in and out of the Centre. We call it restless sleep. Consciousness occurs of bits and pieces, most of which come down from the brain.

More accurately, consciousness keeps rushing to the brain and other centres and down again like a yoyo.

Other bits and pieces come from the staircase (previous lives or astral travelling).

All of these we call dreams. Although the experiences are sometimes very vivid, because our awareness is feeble, things get mixed up. Looking back at our dreams from the waking state, when our awareness is strong, we see that some dreams are trivial, others seem profound and symbolic.

It is from the latter that psychologists like Carl Jung have conceptualised their theories of the Unconscious. However, they didn't actually discover the Centre (they used the wrong tools), so their theorising is a mixture of the obviously true and the obviously not.

BASIC METHOD

Feel your way into it by watching your breathing.

The breathing starts and finishes at the Centre. Feel the breathing carefully and try to locate *exactly* the point at which it stops and starts again.

This is a very pleasant and worthwhile thing to do. The more closely you watch it, the more subtle the breathing becomes. You can *feel* the attention subsiding, sinking down from the brain. Thoughts become weaker, become more easily noted as "thinking" and can be let go of.

As awareness subsides from the throat, there are fewer negative and competitive feelings and emotions. Even those nobler and more agreeable feelings of love and friendship centred in the heart are let go of. The attention focuses increasingly on this tiny centre of our being just above the navel but in the centre of the body.

States of mind and images similar to dreams start to flicker on and off. Since one is doing this deliberately and not just falling asleep one can take care not to let them catapult the attention up to the brain or other secondary centres where they may have come from.

More vigilance is needed to prevent one slipping into sleep (a pleasant state) and losing awareness altogether.

Locating the Centre is like finding the point of balance while standing on a seesaw.

When one finally succeeds, the next step is to sink completely *into* the Centre, withdrawing one's attention from the thinking brain and the outward-looking senses. And stay awake and aware.

When one can do this, one experiences a state, independent of the senses, which is profoundly happy and peaceful. This is the turning point in a man's life.

Repeated experiences will deepen one's awareness of the Centre. One will be increasingly detached from, and free of, the shackles of the body. At this stage one may have out of body experiences with full awareness.

One will be able to watch impulses arise that cause one to reach out into the body-field away from the state of peace. As one understands them, one can bring them under control and eventually stop them altogether.

At this stage one is on the path to salvation and, by

carefully preserving one's awareness and increasing one's knowledge and understanding of the goal, one is assured of ultimate release from suffering and being established in the state of Perfection.

ADVANCED METHOD: *Turning on the Light*

We have been entering a dark cave (the Centre) and trying to *feel* our way back into the origin of ourselves. Darkness and sleep tend to go together. Consequently, we often find ourselves outside the cave again with no recollection (no consciousness) of what happened. We simply fell asleep.

Exploring a cave *can* be done by feeling one's way with one's hands. It is slow. The knowledge one gains is limited. Cave explorers usually take a source of light with them. They see much more. It is easier to understand what one *sees* rather than to rely on feeling alone.

It is more efficient if we can take a light into the Centre. Exploration becomes easier and one doesn't stumble into the darkness of sleep.

Some people see a tiny light when they locate the Centre. This can be expanded and used. Some people don't.

Some people can use the inner eye by which one can see in dreams, when one is asleep with one's eyes closed. Wide-awake, such people can visualise whatever they want to and experience the corresponding emotional response, fear of the tiger, attraction for the pretty girl. It's all a question of one's previous karma. Some people can't.

It *is* possible to train oneself. One looks at a light bulb, a candle or the moon, closes one's eyes and tries to hold on to the after-image. It fades. One opens one's eyes and repeats. It fades. One repeats again and again. Until one is successful. Or one gives up.

If one gives up, one goes back to the basic method. The Basic method works but it takes longer. The Advanced method is Fast-Track.

If one can visualise an image of a lighted sphere, it won't necessarily appear in the Centre. It may appear in front of your face or between your eyes or in your chest or elsewhere. At first it may not be stable. It may flicker or change its form or size. Or disappear altogether.

One practises until one can sustain it in the form of a lighted sphere. Because it is a mental image, it can be manipulated by the mind. It can be moved and changed by the mind once control over it has been gained. One practises until one can make the sphere bigger or smaller at will. Then one tries to move it to other parts of the body. It can be used to illuminate the inside of any part of the body that one moves it to. It can also be used to illuminate the other centres in the body if one wants to investigate their characteristics.

For Fast-Track, one uses it to investigate the Centre. One moves the light exactly to the Centre. This is the equivalent of taking a light to the mouth of a dark cave. The colour of the sphere when illuminating the Centre depends upon the condition of the individual. It can be any colour, including black. The default setting for a being whose morality and character are sound is generally gold or white.

Mara's Centre is red; Satan's is black.

One is now in a position to explore the various levels of reality or home in directly on Nibbāna.

16. EXPLORATION

One makes the lighted sphere a useful size. A golf ball is too small. A tennis ball is probably too small. A small football is good.

Up until now one has been seeing and working with the sphere as though it were outside oneself. The next step is to enter it.

One literally just sinks into it.

Wherever one's awareness was coming from before, now it is *inside the sphere*. If successful, one finds oneself sitting in the sphere.

One looks to see where one is. What form does one have? What clothing is one wearing? What colour is one's skin? Is there anything on one's head? What kind of a seat is one sitting on? Can one hear anything, music or birds singing? One looks to see what feeling or emotions one has.

Some people find it difficult to enter the sphere. How can you enter something which is not only smaller than you but also *inside* you?

There is an alternative. You make the sphere bigger. From the size of a ping-pong ball to that of an orange. From orange to grapefruit to football. It's as though you were inflating a balloon (which in a sense you are). Continue to inflate it until you find yourself *inside* it. It is like being in a large luminous bubble. Or a transparent space capsule. Doing it this way produces a tremendous sense of security and well-being.

Either way, one can stay in this state for almost as long as one wishes. It represents a major step forward in self-development; a type of happiness which is free of the unsatisfactoriness of bodily existence. One feels bright, clear, integrated. One is in the centre of oneself.

If one's goal is exploration, one looks in front and around to see what kind of world one is in. One sees landscapes that can be explored, beings that can be communicated with.

Every movement of exploration is triggered by intention. You get to meet the beings who have been reborn there by *deciding to do so.* Sometimes they can remember how they died elsewhere and what were the causes that led to them being born here. This provides a wonderful lesson in karma.

One learns that this level of reality, although an improvement on material existence on earth, is also impermanent. The beings are born (literally, arise) and when their term runs out, they fall way, to be reborn somewhere else. Between these two events, they are happy. If you explore further you will discover that this is true of all the worlds, all the levels of reality.

When you have finished exploring, you can either move out of the sphere and return to full physical awareness or you can continue.

To continue, you re-establish your awareness of yourself as seated in the sphere. You look into the form you have there to see if there is a centre there too. If there is, you will find that it functions in exactly the same way as the original sphere, except that it is usually a different colour. You can make it bigger or smaller. You can enter it. This you do by sinking your awareness into it as before.

You are now on another plane of reality. Again you look to see what form you have; what kind of seat you are sitting on; what you are wearing; what feelings and sensations you are experiencing; what kind of world you are in; what beings inhabit the place; how they got there; who they had been previously; where they came from.

The limitations to exploration are set by the limits of one's capacity for mental conception and the limits of the band in which one finds oneself. If it occurs to one to look for buildings, one will find them. If not, one may not. One can discover who or what is the presiding deity or guardian of this world and question him too.

Again one discovers that although the life span of these beings is long by our standards, it still has the same characteristics. Beings arise and, after a while, they fall away to arise somewhere else in accordance with their karma.

The beings are happy but their happiness and activities are more refined than on the previous level, which, in its turn, is more refined than physical existence as we know it.

When one is satisfied, one can either return directly to one's normal physical form or one can go on. If you want to go on, you look for the sphere in the centre of the form you have on that plane of existence and enter it as before. You then proceed in exactly the same way to a higher level.

There are many worlds or planes of existence rising higher than ours and they can all be accessed in this way, while one is still alive, starting with the first sphere located in the centre of your physical body.

There are many worlds or planes of existence sinking lower, too, and they can be accessed in the same way.

The higher worlds are levels of increasing fineness and happiness. The lower worlds are levels of increasing coarseness and suffering, hell worlds in fact.

One is free to explore these too but as one explores lower, one experiences landscapes and beings that are more miserable and become horrific. If one's mind is steady, one can communicate with the beings there and find out what actions led to their appearance there. One will gain more insight into how cause and effect (karma) works.

When one is not exploring in this way, one can return to one's present life and see, with new eyes, the way karma is operating here. One begins to see where, based on their current behaviour, beings (including oneself) are likely to be reborn if they do not change.

All these experiences are similar to travelling as a tourist to a foreign country and finding out what it's like there.

If one wants to stay, one discovers that one's tourist visa is not sufficient and one looks to see what conditions one needs to fulfil in order to qualify for long stay there.

So it is with spiritual or mental tourism. With this difference. When a being dies on any level of being, if he does not enter Nibbāna, he will be reborn, not necessarily according to his desires. It is more likely that it will be in accordance with his deserts; either on some other level, or perhaps on the same one. Quite a lot depends on the state and content of one's mind at the moment of death.

Realising this, one can take control of one's destiny and *use* karma. If one wants to arise after death on this or that desirable level of existence, one has to have done this or that in one's present lifetime in order to qualify. One finds out what needs to be done and one tries to do it.

The procedure is no different from finding that, if you want work as a teacher, you need a degree. So you knuckle down and work to get that degree. *While you still have time.*

In both cases, if you satisfy the requirements of the cause - the effect - the job or the favourable rebirth, is inevitable.

One also sees that if one makes no particular effort to prepare for one's future, one is reborn by default but still in accordance with karma.

If one makes no effort to get any kind of education so that one is illiterate, one still *has* to get a job. But it has to be something that one *can* do. So one will probably end up with manual work. If one is of bad character, even the better manual jobs may be out of reach.

Similarly, if one spends one's life fishing, one is likely to arise on a level that is inhabited by fish. One will then be able to experience what fish do, and see life on the other side of the coin.

The world of fish is also a realm that one can visit as a "tourist" while one is still alive if one doubts these things.

If one keeps investigating, one comes to see from experience, or by intuitive understanding, that all levels both high and low have the same characteristics; one arises there, and after a time, long or short, one dies away from there. The more merit, the longer the lifespan.

What determines the location and length of one's lifespan is what in Buddhism is called one's merit (or demerit). An accumulation of good actions results in one arising in a happy realm.

This is like having earned enough to stay in a good hotel. When the money runs out, one has to leave. When the accumulation of good is exhausted, one dies. Those who have accumulated more money or more goodness stay longer. But no-one can stay forever. Not in any world.

In the case of the unhappy realms, it is the accumulation of one's demerits, one's misdeeds, which gets one there. This is similar to a prison sentence. The more serious the crime, the longer the sentence. Once the sentence runs out, one is released to continue one's transmigration through the worlds.

One needs to realise that, though one can choose to commit meritorious or demeritorious actions, one is not free to choose the consequences. A man can choose to jump off a skyscraper. He cannot choose not to hit the street below. A man can choose to commit a crime or not. He cannot choose not to be punished for it. The formula is simple.

Do good, experience all goes well.
Do bad, experience pain in hell.
(*Gnomonic Verses*)

One realises that even the highest and most sublime states of mind and states of being are impermanent.

This resembles a ski slope. In order to ski down, one has to climb up to the top. Again and again. The higher the mountain, the longer the ski run down but, also, the longer the climb up. In the end, one finds all this trudging up higher and higher in order to slide down further and further unsatisfactory.

Every time one wants a birth, one gets a birth all right. But one also gets a death. Always. Everywhere. Even in the highest heavens. Even among the gods.

Using this method of exploration, you can track down the highest gods. You will find that they all have Centres; that they can all be questioned. Although they may exist for what, from our points of view, are unimaginably long periods of time, in the end they all fall away from their power and splendour to some lower level out of which they have arisen. There are no exceptions. In the end, one comes to the conclusion: all this is unsatisfactory.

One comes to want something or somewhere permanent and without disturbance. One wants a state of peace, perfect and unending. One is ready for Nibbāna.

The method for experiencing Nibbāna is straightforward but it requires good concentration and perseverance.

Starting with the first sphere that one established in the centre of one's physical body, one enters this. But, instead of paying any attention to the plane of existence on which one now finds oneself, one looks for a sphere in one's new, finer form. When it has been located, one enters it. Again, resisting the temptation to become interested in this new level of reality, one goes directly to find the lighted sphere in one's new, even finer form.

One continues to do this, sphere to sphere, form to form, moving steadily deeper and deeper into higher and higher, finer and finer realms. Theoretically, there could be an uncountable series of spheres, each more subtle and higher than the one before. In practice, the mind, in its pursuit of ultimate happiness, tends to jump, to make quantum leaps and it is possible to see that the worlds one experiences form groups that have features in common.

Actually, it is one's own mind grasping after these levels which makes one put in an appearance in them at all. Just as, for the tourist, there are innumerable destinations but he makes for the ones that appeal to him. He doesn't have to keep hopping off the train at every single station. (Unless he wants to.)

One's desire for separate existence is what determines how long this process lasts. One's desire for peace speeds it up. One's pursuit of things that catch one's attention prolongs it.

As the desire for peace becomes stronger than the desire for separate existence, the forms get finer and finer until a most extraordinary thing happens. One finds oneself on an incredibly fine and subtle plane where, if one still has a form, it is no longer clothed but shining and transparent. If one can see any level of existence at all, it is without any noticeable characteristic; a vast universal sameness. If one has any feelings, they are unbelievably cool and subtle.

When one goes to continue the process of exploring upwards by locating the sphere in this form, one discovers there isn't one.

One no longer has a Centre.

This is understood by reference to the Universal Octopus. For each tentacle, it is the sphere from which it reached out that is its centre. But in this reverse process of the tentacle subsiding into its centre, the original sphere itself has been reached and the tentacle itself is experienced as this last bright transparent form without a centre. One can hold this position while one contemplates the significance of no centre.

This is the very gate to Nibbāna. When one sees the significance, there is a letting go of all desire for separation, the final form disappears and Nibbāna is experienced and puts an end to any further doubts.

Unless one's lifespan has nearly come to an end, one rarely dies at this point unless there is a strong impulse to do so. One has come here as a tourist. One's physical body still exists. The merit/demerit, which fuels it, has not run out. One is still alive.

Consequently, after a while, one reappears in one's physical body, seeing, hearing, smelling, tasting, touching as before.

One can use one's current mind to review the whole practice and see what traces of attachment to mundane existence remain. One can normally repeat the experience as often as one wants.

Even though one has experienced Nibbāna while one is alive, one will not necessarily enter Parinibbāna (*Final Nibbāna*) when one dies. If there are still attachments in the mind to subtle types of experience which do not involve a physical form, one will be reborn in subtle planes of existence which correspond to these experiences. One will be able to continue one's progress to the Ultimate from there.

If one removes all attachments which stand between oneself and permanent Nibbāna while one is still alive, one simply carries on with one's life, content that, in the end, there will be Parinibbāna. In this case, essentially, whatever one does or does not do, one is waiting for life to run out.

When this happens, the physical body dies in its own time and there is no more coming and going. One reaches the stage of Parinibbāna. This is no different from the Nibbāna one has already experienced once or many times as a tourist. Except that now one does not again leave it.

There have always been those who do not want to wait until the natural end of their lifespan. They either allow the body to die by no longer feeding it or end its life prematurely.

Even in the Buddha's time there were monks who "took the knife", that is killed themselves, in order to enter Parinibbāna.

When questioned about this, the Buddha said there was nothing wrong in what they had done. They were Arahants and were entitled to do it. But he discouraged it as it led to misunderstandings in the minds of ordinary people and, as it were, tended to give the Sangha (the Order of Monks) a bad name.

There have also always been those who, having come to the end of all attachment to separate existence on all levels, develop the ability to leave at will. They simply choose to leave and, if there is absolutely no substratum of attachment, they never come back.

In doing this, they are also able to <u>choose</u> the date and time of their departure.

17. THE CENTRE AS SOURCE

Put your hand over the Centre. You can do this in any position. The easiest is lying down. But this is also the easiest position in which to fall asleep since the effect is agreeable and calming. You can do it standing or walking. If you look at pictures of Napoleon, you will see that he even did it on horseback. But for our purposes the most convenient posture is sitting down.

Your hand is covering your stomach. It is also covering the centre of the universe and the source of everything that has ever been or will be. The potentiality is infinite. If you think this thought, while your hand is there, it concentrates the mind wonderfully and you may get a feeling that your body hair is standing on end and a chill passes over the surface of your skin. It will occur to you that *anything is possible.* Not just in general, though that is true, but possible for *you.*

It is like Aladdin discovering his lamp.

But how to use it? Although the source is capable of bringing anything or any circumstances into existence, it is itself entirely non-active. It is purely reactive.

This can be understood if we consider the history of electricity. Electricity has existed for millions and millions of years. Egyptian texts from 2750 BC refer to electric fish giving people shocks. But it was not until the nineteenth century that the human brain started to produce ideas that enabled this source of energy to be harnessed. Now it powers entertainment, transport, heating, lighting, communication and computation and has revolutionised the modern world. But although electricity is the source of the power, it does nothing of itself. It is the mind, which comes up with ideas as to *how* it might be used, that harnesses that power.

Consider: an electric circuit travels around your room in a plastic cable. It's there. It flows. But that's all. It doesn't do anything else. It doesn't warm or cool you, or light the room or provide pictures of what is going on in other parts of the world or play Mozart or drill holes in your walls or heat your bathwater or boil your kettle.

To achieve any of these things, *you* have to invent (or buy) some kind of machine or appliance and then find a way of getting the electricity to flow through it and accomplish what you want.

And it is invisible. As a newcomer to the world (a young child), the only sense you could contact it with is *touch* and your parents take precautions to prevent your doing this. So until your parents or teachers tell you about it and explain how it works, you have no idea of its existence. Even if you did manage to get your fingers on it, you would have no idea what happened to you.

So it is with the Centre. It's there. It is the source of everything imaginable (including electricity). You would not be alive or reading this or have a past and a future if it were not because of this source. Yet, in itself, it is completely non-active. It initiates nothing. It is passively peaceful. Yet it can *potentially* produce everything. But to produce *anything,* it needs a sustained thought to harness it.

It is the horse standing patiently (and contentedly) waiting for a rider to motivate it in a given direction. It is the lamp waiting for Aladdin to wipe off the dust and express a wish or intention. You are the rider. You are Aladdin.

Because it is non-active, it is non-partisan. It is completely neutral. It can be used to paint a picture (or produce a painter). It can be used to make an electric chair. Electricity can keep you alive in a Siberian winter or kill you if you peel off the cable with your fingers.

Because the Centre is non-active and invisible, it cannot be heard or smelt or tasted or touched. Therefore, ordinarily, men are unaware of its existence. Yet *because* of it, we see, hear, smell, taste, touch and think, build our worlds and live and die.

How is it that something that is non-active can produce a whole universe? Because it's non-activity doesn't mean it is nothing. On the contrary, its infinite potentiality means that it can provide anything in response to circumstances. As a piece of plasticine can be moulded into any desired shape; as iron can be cast as a gate or tempered to be a sword.

The circumstances to which it responds are primarily mental impulses. Concepts accompanied by intentions. The intention is the equivalent of the electric cable that links the generator to the appliance. The appliance at origin appears as a concept in mind.

For example, Edison conceived the idea of an instrument that could record and reproduce sound. He sketched it on a piece of paper and gave it to his assistant with the instruction, "Make this!" The result was the first tinfoil phonograph. The idea was Edison's, as was the intention that passed it on to the assistant. The materials used were already existing, having, at some stage, been the product of previous intentions. The whole production was the response of the Source to this process.

So this source, this Centre, is what *your* hand is covering, when you put it on your stomach and cover your navel. It's in there somewhere. So small, that it won't show up on an x-ray. So potent, that it will power an atomic bomb.

Initially, attempts to locate something that is a gateway to non-matter involve tracking the breathing. Because the breath, which is the sustainer of the life of the body, is palpable but also very subtle. It begins each time at the Centre and ends at the Centre. It is the link between the temporary, the human being that lives and dies, and the Eternal, which, having had no beginning, has no end.

Focusing the attention on the breath for this purpose results in the breath becoming finer and this fineness enables the mind, which is non-material (it is the brain which is material), to become aware of the *presence* of the Centre.

The Centre, while remaining itself non-active, is constantly the source of reactions to circumstances and, as it were, sends back responses.

Because your hand acts as a kind of energy shield, it reflects back and magnifies the stream of vibrations which intermittently come out from the direction of the Centre. The hand itself heats up and feels like a battery that has been recharged. If you move your hand to a part of the body where there is a feeling of discomfort, you might experience instant relief.

This energy is also perceived as feelings that originate at the gateway and turbulate around the gateway. Sometimes, they are strong enough to travel up and engage the higher, secondary centres or, of course, down to the lower ones. (See Chart A Chapter 25).

These feelings tell us a great deal about the Centre and a great deal about ourselves.

Firstly, they help locate the Centre. It is the opposite of looking for the centre of a whirlpool. With a whirlpool you follow the rings of water to the point where they disappear *into* its centre. With the Centre you track back everything to where it comes *out of* the Centre. When you get past the turbulence to the Centre itself, you experience a complete unmoving stillness.

This affects your whole body. All the stress and tension and activity in it and in the subsidiary centres (above and below) cease. You feel as though you are on the edge of an enormous Silence.

The feelings also help us to become aware of the kind of people we are, the kind of things we get up to and the true significance of the things that go on around us.

Firstly, ourselves: every time you experience a feeling around the Centre that is agreeable, if you are alert, can you instantly associate it with something you have done, are doing or thinking? If you have a happy, positive, outgoing thought about someone or something you like, the feeling is within the spectrum of pleasure. The Centre is reflecting back your goodness.

Every time you experience a feeling of discomfort (not indigestion!) emanating in this area, can you associate it with something you have done, are doing or thinking? Negative states of mind, thoughts, intentions and actions are reflected back as discomfort or pain. The intensity of them is consistent with the seriousness of what you are doing.

A small boy who is about to kill his first rabbit or fish feels very strong reactions which would often be sufficient to dissuade him if he did not allow himself to be persuaded by peer pressure (or perhaps hunger).

The radiation from the Centre, which is non-dualistic in nature, reflects back, from the point of view of non-duality, your mental activities. It is a mirror image. That's why karma is so perfect. If you put out negativity, you get back negativity.

At first, it is perceived in the area around the Centre in your physical body. If this does not cause you to reassess, the negativity, *your* negativity, spreads up to the other centres. There is pain in the Heart Chakra, conflict in the Throat Chakra and a proliferation of thinking in the Brain Chakra. It affects the physical body. You become unwell. It ripples out into your environment. People don't like you. It reaches your whole world. Your world becomes a mess.

Since everything is a unity,

negativity to any one of the tentacles is negativity towards the whole octopus and each and every one of its tentacles. Just as punching someone on the jaw is a hostile act to the whole person, not just to an individual bone.

Those who are persistently resistant to the way the Centre mirrors their characters and refuse to change increasingly have problems in the area where the Centre is located and often end up with serious stomach problems.

They try to deal with these by treating the *physical* symptoms with drugs (legal or otherwise), alcohol or just plain old-fashioned over-eating.

Building up a mountain of fat around the Centre is an attempt to desensitise awareness in that area. But then it also desensitises awareness elsewhere. Often these attempts to shut out what can be seen as messages from the Centre or the workings of conscience result in cancer.

If you are thinking funny thoughts, you will laugh. See if the laughter is coming from the Centre. All genuine laughter comes from the Centre. This sort of laughter is contagious because we all have the Centre in common. Laughter from the heart can be contagious, too.

Laughter from the throat or brain is not. It is not really laughter. It sounds more like a scream. There is no humour in it. It is separateness revealing itself. It is an expression of pain.

The feelings also help us to become aware of the true significance of the things that go on around us. Things that we *don't* originate.

If you keep your hand on your stomach and maintain awareness of the Centre when you are with people or other beings, you will sometimes experience feelings of unease or even something stronger. This can be because the beings you are with are not genuine or may even be hostile to you, but concealing it. Their words or body language may be friendly, but you discover that you doubt them or distrust them.

I am a patch of sunshine on the path
(said the tiger)
dappled and hard to see.

The forest is quiet and waiting
(said the tiger)
no need for fear of me.
(Blondin)

Sometimes people call this intuition. It is the Centre reflecting back what the beings *are* rather than what they appear to be.

No matter what the label may be,
by its fruit we judge the tree.

This is common with young children before they have become corrupted by the standards of the adults around them. They are very much in touch with the Centre and are instinctively guided by the way it reflects back the people and world around them. They need to be. For survival.

"Don't be silly, Alex, come and say hello to the Minister! Alex! I'm so sorry, Minister, he's not usually shy like this. (Just you wait till I get you home!)"

One pays attention to the clear emanations from the Centre. They take on the colour of what is being thought, said or done. These activities thereby become perceptible.

They are seen for what they really are, rather than how they are presented. One becomes more skilled at differentiating between what is good and what is bad. One aligns oneself more and more with the non-dualistic, and therefore impartial, Centre and source. One is protected by the non-dualistic nature of the Centre by receiving direct understanding of people's characters and motives because one shares a common source with them. This is an example of upstreaming, which can go on all the time in everyday life. (See chapter 22).

This results in a much better life. One's relations with other forms of life, including people, are normalised because one puts an end to hostile activities of thought, word and deed towards them.

The feelings which turbulate around the Centre often reveal conflict within oneself.

There is what one has been taught and seems required to do by conditioning; *kill that rabbit!* And there is the uncorrupted response from the Centre; *it doesn't want to suffer, just as you don't.*

Both have their origins in the secondary centres and are based on responses to contacts at the sense doors and the feeling linked to those contacts.

In this the brain is involved. It organises the data received from sense contacts and, from these data, produces points of view.

The senses from which the brain gets its data are

fundamentally dualistic; eye and object of sight; ear and sound; nose and smell; tongue and taste; skin and touch-contact.

Computers themselves (and therefore brains) operate with dualities (on/off switches). They cannot comprehend or handle the concept of Oneness. If you investigate the Brain Chakra with the lighted sphere (see chapter 24), you meet question and answer; pros and cons; thesis and antithesis; past and present; postulates, deductions, inductions, conclusions; debate; the continuous juggling of thoughts which derive from data obtained at the sense doors. This is a process endlessly creating points of view. These are endlessly liable to modification.

Points of view trigger off feelings and, if these are significant enough, they cause speech and action. Speech and actions affect others and, in so far as others are tentacles (see chapter 8), impinge upon the Centre itself. Once a point of view is in place, it tends to attract data that support it. This continues until sufficient momentum is built up for action to be taken.

I see a tiger. The brain/computer checks the data it has on tigers and produces a deduction that it is a threat to survival. This gets my pulses racing and I am afraid for my life. I waver somewhere within the range of caution and flight.

The brain/computer is quite neutral, however, and if new data is introduced it will, unless overruled by a fixed viewpoint, adjust its conclusion, just as a number, introduced into a column of figures, adjusts the total automatically.

The tiger is getting closer. The new deduction is, "Do something urgently!"

The "tiger" is seen to be a man dressed up. The new deduction is, "Find out what that man is up to." (The tiger has now disappeared.)

18. HEALING

If one has a health problem, the first thing is to locate the exact point of the feeling of discomfort. It's not sufficient to say, 'my foot hurts' or 'I've got indigestion' or 'there's something wrong with my liver' or 'I have migraine'. These are just thoughts. They may correspond to facts but you can't *do* anything with them except breed more thoughts.

In order to deal with pain from *inside* and put things right, you have to upstream thoughts and labels. You have to focus on the actual experience of pain. The feeling. And exactly where it is. This is what you work with.

If you can use the lighted sphere, you illuminate the point of feeling and the area in which it occurs. You may be able to see with the inner eye what is wrong. You may not. In either case, the treatment is the same. You establish the lighted sphere in the Centre.

You mentally draw up a column of light to where it hurts as a continuous stream of energy. You can use the in breath as a kind of pump. It is a bit like sucking up water until you can get it to flow to a higher level as a continuous flow.

The intention is to surround and infuse the place where it hurts; to saturate it. Mentally, you can adjust this stream of light so that you not only *see* it, but also *feel* it as something warm and healing. You can make it feel relaxing. You can cause it to vibrate.

You feel it penetrating the area of discomfort. You look for shadows or dark spots and erase them with light. You can increase the brightness of the light and consequently the intensity of the healing. You continue this until the discomfort ceases and there is no trace of shadow or darkness. If, later, it recurs, you repeat the process until it never comes back.

You can use the same method to deal with tiredness, stress, aching or any kind of discomfort in the head. You draw the light up as a fountain and fill the whole of the inside of the head with warm, healing light. You look for shadows or areas of darkness or centres of tension and use the light to dispel them.

You can also try this. Use the sphere to activate the Centre. Then *move* the sphere until it entirely encloses the affected area. Then gradually turn up the volume of light, warmth and relaxing vibrations until the discomfort disappears.

You may not have thought of hunger as something that might need healing. You may think, if it does, that the cure is obviously eating! But there are situations where food is not available or one is trying to diet and becomes subject to extreme craving.

In these cases, home in on the *feeling* and its exact location. Enclose it with the lighted sphere and generate light, warmth, relaxation and peace until the hungry feeling goes away. It *always* goes away.

This is an easy way to give up smoking. If you follow the instructions every time you feel an urge to smoke. Locate the *feeling*. Enclose it in the sphere. Generate light, warmth, relaxation and peace. You need never smoke again. Of course it will work with drugs, alcohol or even lusting after your neighbour's wife (which is, morally, worse even than opium!).

If you can't use the light, it can be done just with feeling instead. You feel where the pain is as accurately as you can and you draw up a feeling of flowing warmth and healing from the Centre.

As an extension of this you can do periodic health checks on yourself. You expand the lighted sphere until it fills the whole of the inside of the body, torso, head, arms, legs, hands, feet, senses (eyes, ears etc.). It is just like filling up a balloon with air.

You then carefully and patiently examine every part, every corner, for feelings of discomfort and dark patches. These you illuminate by intensifying the light in that place until the symptoms disappear.

A further extension is the Rejuvenation Cycle.

If you are feeling fine and seem to have nothing obviously wrong with you, you can build on this. You direct a flow of warm, healing light from the Centre into the various parts of the body, one at a time; eyes, chest, throat, lungs, feet etc. You mentally focus on it as *penetrating* the part, saturating it. The idea is not just to bathe e.g. the eyes, but to get the light and accompanying warm and nourishing feelings to seep into the very cells themselves, the molecules, the atoms. And renew them.

An alternative method is to (mentally) divide the body into zones. Start with the area between the navel and the crotch (to include the pelvis and genitalia). Move the lighted sphere there and use it to fill the whole area with light, warmth and vibration. Get the light to soak into the cells. Do this until the whole area feels light and clean and healthy. Then repeat in the area between the navel and the throat.

Use the breathing-in to inflate the chest with the light. Next, repeat with the head. Ensure that everything in the head, including the eyes, ears, forehead, jaws and the inside of the mouth, is relaxed and without tension. The more you can get the light into the cells and molecules, the more you can *feel* the success of what you are doing.

Of course the body is doing this all the time. Cells are constantly being renewed. But normally the overall quality of natural regeneration declines in line with the natural deterioration of the body through ageing.

In this case, we are upstreaming what the body has been programmed to do naturally and introducing rejuvenation more directly from the infinite potential of the source itself.

And we are doing it consciously and intentionally, using the principle that "mind comes first". From the point of view of conventional dualistic thinking operating in the brain, we are performing miracles. But a "miracle" is just one of a pair of dualities: things which occur normally and which *can* be explained satisfactorily within the constraints of current known ("scientific") opinion; and things that *seem* to occur and *cannot* be explained satisfactorily within current opinion.

From the point of view of the Centre, there are no miracles. Everything can be explained on the basis that everything in existence has *come from* the one source and, therefore, anything is possible. All that is needed is for mind to conceive it, confidently find out *how* and diligently *do* it.

Technically, there seems to be no limit to how far you can go with this (see chapter 32). You are after all using the source of everything in the universe. How far a given individual, such as yourself, can go depends on how good you get at the practice.

Consider: it was known for hundreds of years that it was possible to swim the English Channel. The fact that it had never been done didn't mean it was impossible. Just that there hadn't been swimmers good enough and confident enough to do it. Then along came Captain Matthew Webb on August 25th 1875 and did it. Since then, of course, there have been many others. Nowadays you get swimmers who can swim across to France and back again the same day. There is no limit.

Anything is possible. You just have to conceptualise it (have the idea), work out how and then apply sustained effort. Mostly, the doing of it depends on *believing* that the Centre really is what it is; the limitless source of everything in the universe.

19. HEALING OTHERS

If you cover the Centre with your hand as a kind of shield, your hand will become aware of a subtle radiation, which will cause the hand to feel as though it has taken on a charge like a battery. If you move it to another part of your body, it will discharge. If there is discomfort there, this will relax and disappear.

This indicates the possibilities of healing others. It has been called "the laying on of hands". When a child is hurt, it can be pacified almost instantly if its mother touches the place. Provided the contact between mother and child has not been broken.

People who can do this significantly are called healers. They will usually tell you that they are not themselves doing the healing. Rather they are making themselves available so that a greater benign force can flow through them and heal. This force comes from the Centre, sometimes via the Heart Chakra.

If you can work with the light sphere, you can try making (with your mind – mind comes first) the flow of light pass from the Centre, out through your hand and into the affected part of your friend. Exactly the same as when you practised self-healing on yourself. You may even be able to see inside your friend's body while you are doing this.

Since with the Centre anything is possible, it is clear that it is possible to dispense with the physical contact or even the need to be physically present with the other person. By entering the Centre in your own body, it is possible to contact the other and use the lighted sphere to act directly on and in his body by means of visualisation.

This is healing from a distance.

You are effectively upstreaming the physical difference and separateness of your two bodies.

It is a matter of two tentacles interacting with each other *via their common centre.*

This indicates the main obstacle. Firstly, the healer must be able to access the power of the Centre. Secondly, there must be no obstacle between the sick man and the same Centre.

Ignorance is not an obstacle. Seriously negative acts towards other tentacles – killing, betrayal – are an obstacle.

This is why theistic religions insist on repentance before forgiveness and healing can take place.

Both healer and patient have to meet at their common Centre so that the flow of healing can occur.

Non-repentance is an act of will. It is a refusal; a refusal to see that one has done serious wrong; a refusal to put it right; and therefore a refusal to do what needs to be done to be healed.

You cannot heal someone against his will.

20. HOSTILITY AND FEAR

The beam of light from a torch is empty. Because of it, objects become illuminated and visible.

The radiation from the Centre is colourless and neutral. Because of it, feelings of happiness and unhappiness, joy, fear, hostility etc. are perceived turbulating around the Centre.

The Centre does not act, it reacts. Mind comes first. Thinking causes a reaction. In terms of feelings around the Centre, it works like this: if I have a good thought, I feel good. If I think bad, I feel bad, uncomfortable.

Hostility and fear start as thoughts directed towards another in my mind. This will provoke feelings that correspond to these thoughts. They won't be peaceful and harmonious feelings. If you sow carrot seed you get carrots, you don't get parsnips.

Sow hostility; you get hot, disturbed, violent, restless feelings which produce more thoughts and images of the same kind and act like fuel on a fire. This builds up until there is a powerful urge to release the pressure by doing something. I speak; I act in accordance with this build-up of hostility. The people around me, the world outside me, repay me in kind.

Sow fear and you get feelings that reflect your vulnerability to people, forces and events which are hostile to you and whose power you feel unable to resist. These feelings produce more images and thoughts of the same kind.

The feeling of weakness and vulnerability builds up and seems to threaten your very survival. It can reach a pitch where, in order to survive, you either run or make a pre-emptive strike. Or your feeling of weakness in the face of what you perceive to be an overwhelming threat predominates and you become paralysed. Like the rabbit, frozen with fear, waiting for the stoat to come and kill it.

All of this is like standing in your own shadow and wondering why it is dark.

The "cure" for feelings of discomfort around the Centre arising from hostile thoughts is to see if one is originating them and, if so, stop.

21. HOSTILITY FROM OTHERS

Sometimes one has feelings of discomfort around the Centre, which one interprets as hostility or fear. Closer investigation shows that they have not originated in one's thinking. One's computer/brain has simply registered feelings originating elsewhere and *interpreted* them as hostility.

In fact, someone else is having hostile thoughts or intentions, possibly directed at you. The ability to become aware of the hostile or deceptive intentions of others is a self-protection mechanism made possible by the nature of the Centre.

The answer is to ensure that one is not triggered off into viewpoints about others that will lead to similar reactive feelings in oneself. Otherwise, one may retaliate.

It is possible to react to those who verbally and physically abuse one without negativity and generate thoughts that are friendly.

However, if one puts one's attention right in the Centre, this will upstream everything so that even the awareness of what he is up to will fade away. One just sees him for what he really is; a suffering being.

22. UPSTREAMING

It has tended to become habitual for modern man to try to solve the problems encountered in life on the human level of existence by using the brain and its thinking. Often this works. But when the brain can't solve a problem, one needs to look somewhere else for a solution.

If you type into a sophisticated computer 'I am thirsty', you can get it to come up with innumerable kinds of drinks and permutations of drinks, suggestions for vessels to put them in, places to buy them and information about their vitamin and mineral content.

But this doesn't quench your thirst any more than reading hundreds of menus will satisfy your hunger. It just gives you more to think about. It will probably make you *thirstier*.

Once you realise this, you see that if you want to put an end to your thirst, you have to do something in a different dimension. Outside of your computer.

You have to get up and go to the fridge and start putting liquids into your mouth.

This is an example of upstreaming.

Imagine a river flowing down onto a wide area of lowland, a delta. Here it spreads out into small streams. The problem this creates in the delta is that the ground tends to become waterlogged and marshy, particularly in the rainy season. If there are houses in the delta, they get flooded. We can try rerouting the local streams that affect the houses nearby. But this causes neighbouring streams to fill up more and they may overflow. Blocking up these causes more water to build up in other parts of the delta where there is already a flooding problem.

We need to go further upstream, tracing the smaller streams to where they branch off from larger streams and reroute the water there. If this doesn't work because the water is still entering the delta elsewhere, we might decide on a more drastic solution. Trace all the streams, great or small, back until we reach the river itself from which they all obtain water. Then we might build a great dam, which would enable us to reroute the whole river so that it ultimately reaches the sea without entering the delta at all.

This will solve it. The marshland dries out and can be easily drained. End of problem.

Or consider this early version of the Greek tale of the Hydra that lived in Lake Lema and terrorised the villagers. The Hydra was a monster with many heads. If one head was cut off, two others grew in its place. So any attempt to get rid of the monster only made matters worse.

When Herakles was given the task of killing it, he saw that all the heads came from a single neck. He told his nephew Iolaus to get a flaming firebrand. Then he cut off the neck of the monster, upstream of all the heads, and used the firebrand to cauterise the wound.

If you can't get a refund for your airline ticket from the girl at the desk no matter how much you argue and threaten her, you have to go upstream in the chain of command until you reach someone who actually has the power to say yes. Or no.

These are all examples of upstreaming. Something can't be solved on its own level? You trace it back to a higher level.

So it is with the computer/brain. If it can't produce thoughts which provide a solution that makes the problem disappear, one needs to upstream and seek a solution elsewhere.

In the present world situation, this step has been forgotten. Individuals, scientists, governments go on and on producing more and more thoughts which, instead of providing solutions, contribute to the problems. Or even create new ones.

The same principle holds good on the fundamental level. We need to go upstream to an earlier centre.

If you have a relationship that has been established in the Heart Chakra and it slips out of this zone, what do you do? For example, your marriage is on the rocks.

Your first attempt is to solve it in the head. You talk things over. You are reasonable. You consider the children, the house, the bank account, the need to listen more, to be more understanding, less selfish. The computer can continue to produce data until its electricity supply is cut off or it crashes. But it all boils down to *thoughts* about what went wrong, how and when, and what can be done about it.

If this works, that's fine. You slip back into the Heart zone and normal happiness resumes. But if the thinking and talking goes on without getting anywhere; if you reach agreement today and it all starts going wrong again tomorrow; then you have to upstream.

If you upstream from the Brain to the Throat, positions

and attitudes harden. In this zone, dualistic attitudes are fixed. It becomes an increasingly bitter struggle to prove who was right and who was wrong, who will get custody of the children, who will get more of the money (if there is any). It can be a terminal struggle. In one case known to me, the wife waited until her unfaithful husband fell asleep and then poured petrol on him and set him alight. To prove she was right.

If you are able to upstream it to the Heart, you can re-establish the basis of a loving and friendly relationship, separate but sharing, together but independent, with a strong bonding of affection for another who is like you but also different.

However, if the relationship has involved betrayal in some way, this may not work. Betrayal of another person is also betrayal of the Centre. This fixes the duality in place and prevents upstreaming. In this case, it will revert to the Throat Chakra and become combative; and then to the Brain which will produce an unending stream of thoughts and images for the combatants. These act like fuel and keep the fires burning until either there is an explosion that blows the relationship apart, or the human beings become mentally and emotionally exhausted and drift apart forever.

Why don't we take the further step of upstreaming our problems to the original Centre or indeed go straight there and leave out the later, intermediate, subsidiary ones?

For one thing we don't *know* about it. As homo sapiens, our awareness is tied to "sapiens", *wise* from knowledge obtained by looking outwards through the senses at this world. It is a world made up of things seen, heard, smelled, tasted, touched and thought about. And all these perceptions are stored and processed in the brain.

If you had spent your whole life looking out of a window from a fixed position, unable to move your head or turn your body round, you would be unaware of the room behind you. You would have no idea of how to turn round and see what is there and explore it.

A man who is stone deaf is unaware of that dimension of life which is hearing, because he doesn't have the necessary faculty to access it. And he wouldn't know how to acquire one even if he wanted to.

So it is with the Centre. The Centre is primary, the original, the gateway between your present life and what you were and where you came from. Because it cannot be experienced by smelling, hearing, tasting, touching or thinking, we don't know that it's there. Just as you can't see oxygen if you look out of the window, not even with your glasses on. In fact you didn't know there was anything called "oxygen" until some teacher told you. And you chose to believe him.

The tools of your present life, your senses, are not normally suitable for contacting the Centre. A deaf man cannot hear a Chopin mazurka. (Nor can he see, taste, smell or touch it.)

But because the Centre is the origin of the other centres, it *can* provide solutions to problems which they cannot handle. So if we know about it, we can use it.

Withdrawing our attention from the brain, by putting one's hand on one's stomach so as to cover the navel, is a basic method of upstreaming which one can use in any situation. The breathing becomes more peaceful. The heartbeat slows. One feels one's way into an awareness of the Centre. Awareness is drawn down from the brain.

Someone who has no conscious knowledge of the Centre says of a problem that seems insoluble, "I'll sleep on it!" His instinct is sound. Forget the whole thing. Come back later and refreshed and look at it anew.

All problems exist within the zones of the secondary, later centres. All problems are resolved by withdrawing from them. Most problems involve the computer/brain.

Problems consist of situations where there is a duality.
Or plurality.

Two or more tentacles get trapped in concepts of separateness.

These concepts are about self and others. The "others" can be people, animals or other forms of life, places or things.

The data is in the brain and reveals itself as thoughts and images. If the brain cannot come up with a solution fairly soon, it means it can't be solved in computer terms and you just experience an unending stream of thought.

Just as the computer can't cure your thirst but goes on making suggestions until you get tired of an unending stream of *pictures* of drinks and get up and walk to the fridge.

The reason is that all problems involve the reconciliation of dualities (all computers are basically lots of on/off switches). And if the dualities are irreconcilable as they stand, it means you have to upstream to a point *before* the dualities diverged and produced a concept of separateness that seems to freeze into place.

When one withdraws into the Centre, all dualities disappear.

It happens sometimes with a man-made computer. It seems to get stuck. One does all the obvious things listed under HELP! Then one tries turning it off, waiting five minutes and turning it back on again. Often that solves it.

With the Centre, that always solves it. All problems rest in duality. In the Centre there is no duality. Therefore, the problem doesn't exist. When something doesn't exist, it has been truly solved.

When you look at the problem *from* the Centre, you are looking at it in present time. All computer data is past, things that have already happened. Or predictions about the future, which are based on past data. The past can be revisited and looked at from different points of view but it cannot be changed because it no longer exists. The future hasn't yet come and, by the time it does, the data that was used to predict it may be out of date.

Looking at something from the Centre means looking at something from the centre and source of the universe out of which everything, however unlikely, has actually come. If you had looked at the swirling dense cloud of cooling gases, which was the beginning of this planet, could you have predicted television or bicycles or football matches?

But everything that has emerged from the source actually *did* emerge. Anything is possible. It is only thinking that says it isn't. If you think it isn't possible, you get stuck with that. If you realise that anything *is* possible, then, as soon as you have conceived it, you go out and investigate *how*. You use karma, cause and effect. And it happens.

On the material plane, in this world, some things take longer than others. The boy who heard that acorns produce oak trees planted his acorn and went off. A week later, he came back to see his oak tree. "It doesn't work," he said.

He was wrong. It does work. Anything *is* possible.

PART THREE

HOW EVERYTHING WORKS
AND
WHAT IT CAN ACHIEVE

... all the days of Methuselah were nine hundred sixty and nine years: and he died.

23. CHAKRAS

There is the original Centre. As the outward push from the Centre into the creation and perception of matter developed (see chapters 8 & 13), subsidiary centres appeared, each vitalising and controlling a specific physical area in the body.

It was a colonisation of matter and these subsidiary centres are outposts of the Centre (see page 133). Most of the main ones are in a straight line vertically in the middle of the body.

About two fingers' width below the Centre is a subsidiary centre at the solar plexus. Indians call it manipura. This is linked to all the major centres located above and below it in the human body by the sushumnā. (See Chart A, 133). From the point of view of the material plane, it is the first and most important chakra to develop because it introduces the vital heat which makes possible the metabolism, which the human body uses to maintain a homeostatic temperature. The **Solar Plexus Chakra** is the vehicle by which the non-material light and energy from the Centre is changed into heat. This enables the food that comes into the body to be burned so that nervous and physical energy and strength are distributed throughout the body. You can focus your attention on this centre and locate the source of the vital heat by feeling. Using the mind, you can increase this heat.

The first secondary centre above the Solar Plexus Centre is the Heart. The second is the Throat. The Brain is number three.

The **Heart Chakra** corresponds to:

There is duality but it is the benign duality of self/other recognition.

It is a positive perception which gives rise to all kinds of wholesome feelings such as love, sympathy, empathy (I can feel your pain), compassion (let me help you!), sympathetic joy (I'm really glad you won!), friendliness. All the best relationships dwell in this zone and one experiences a warm (sometimes blissful) feeling in one's chest.

When two or more people are in this zone together, there are no problems that cannot be solved, irrespective of any computer data from the brain that "proves" that the relationship is unsuitable. A relationship centred here is very powerful indeed. It is as though two tentacles had reunited at their outward extremities.

Although still dualistic (they have diverged), they are also one (they have reunited). This is exactly what lovers (including Platonic ones) actually feel. Before everything goes wrong, they really feel they can take on the whole world. Which they often have to.

The **Throat Chakra** is later than the Heart Centre but earlier than the Brain Chakra. Therefore, it is more fundamental in its approach.

You will find that it doesn't work like the brain, storing and analysing data and trying to come to logical conclusions. It is really a combative zone and offers confrontational either/or solutions: winner/loser; mine/yours; master/servant.

The **Brain Chakra** is located in the centre of the head in line with the spot between the eyebrows. It is a computer. It saves and evaluates information collected at the sense doors (including the mind sense door). Consequently, it cannot handle anything that is not dualistic.

Like any other computer, its conclusions are only as good as the data that are fed into it and the programs that handle the data.

"Program" comes from the Greek πρόγραμμα, προ (pro) *before*, γράμμα (gramma) *letter, writing*. Programs are the frameworks and templates which are put into place *before* the data which are to be evaluated. Conclusions arrived at will always, therefore, be within the parameters of these frameworks.

In ordinary language, these programs appear often as points of view, which evaluate the data selectively. They therefore provide limits to the logical functioning of the computer (the computer cannot do anything outside their boundaries).

The fundamental program in human beings, and living beings generally, is SURVIVE!

This means survival as something separate, which is dualistic. Almost all data in the brain's memory banks are evaluated as to whether they are pro-survival or anti-survival. This determines the point of view that arises when realities in the outside world, to which ideas correspond, appear. The point of view determines the response that is given to these realities.

A large cat, nine-foot-long, is seen strolling in the garden. After reference to the memory banks, it is labelled "tiger". The *point of view* is assessed as anti- (my) survival. The *response* to this is running into the house, locking the door and picking up the phone.

Like any other computer, the brain is vulnerable to invasions by the equivalents of viruses and malware. These produce, as it were, *anti-*programs.

They can come via sense contact, especially pleasure and pain that produce feelings. The feelings seem to indicate whether the sense object perceived is pro- or anti- survival.

These indications may not in fact be reliable.

Initial experience of drugs comes into this category. Drugs often produce feelings of well-being in the beginning. Later effects are obviously anti-survival. But by the time this point is reached and a new conclusion evolves, the damage has already been done. It's like the Trojan Horse. A prized spoil of war, once inside the city walls, opens up and out flood enemy soldiers.

Anti-programs can also come through the mind sense door in the form of education, propaganda and advertising. These are often just interchangeable terms that depend upon points of view.

One man's candy crunch may be another man's tooth decay.

One man's Holy War is another man's Mass Murder.

There is another centre located between the eyebrows. It is level with the Brain Chakra and a derivative of it. It therefore came later. It has been called the **Third-Eye Chakra**. It is not active in all men. It is also dualistic. It puts out a subtle vibration of power and, where it is active in someone, it tends to arouse feelings of awe in others if they become aware of it (usually subconsciously).

There is a connection between this centre and the ordinary eyes. The Third-Eye is earlier than the eyes. It developed as the outward push into fine material separateness led to a desire for contact on that level (see chapter 8, first picture). Later, the mind pushed further out and down into the material world of tangible things on the level of the four elements and developed physical eyes to perceive them.

The Third-Eye exists now mainly as a means of contacting

things beyond the individual's five senses. This means you can see (and hear and smell and taste and touch) people and places that your five senses cannot. This will be either because they are on a plane not contactable by the five senses (e.g. heaven worlds) or because they are not within the range of the material senses (too far away).

Not only can you contact them passively, i.e. just perceiving them, but it is also possible to contact them *actively*. For example, you can communicate *to* them. They may not be aware where the communication comes from. Unless they hear your voice, they are likely to assume that it is their own thoughts.

You can also appear *to* them. That is, you can make them see you even though you are not in their presence. When you do this, the form you have, and which they will perceive, is the form which goes with the level you are on. But since it is mind-made, it can be changed at will. When you call up someone you have known before, they may not recognise you unless you adopt a form familiar to them.

This applies both to beings on non-material levels of existence and those in this world.

When you contact beings in this way, you can benefit them by directing good thoughts and intentions towards them. These will produce a wave of happiness that will seem to *arise* in them. Which of course it does.

One may be doing this kind of thing, without realising, every time one has a pleasant thought about someone or somewhere. But such positive impulses are normally weak and fleeting. The *conscious* use of this centre to transmit positive vibrations to a specific recipient or place, or indeed to the whole world, is a powerful tool.

Technically, although it acts by contacting people or places beyond the range of the five senses, it often relies upon information previously obtained through the five senses and stored in the brain. If you did not know that you had an Aunt Mary, how would you go about visualising her and contacting her?

Actions generally need a mental concept before you can do something and the mental concept is likely to be connected with a previously experienced sense object. You want an apple so you go to a tree or a shop. If you had never heard of an apple, you would have to go without.

It is, however, *possible* to use this centre to contact things which are outside the range of your senses, and also of which you have no stored knowledge or memory. For an individual, this really is breaking new ground, exploring uncharted territory.

It is done by going off in a *direction*, rather than towards a destination. Psychologically, directions, in this sense, do not need to be already recorded in the brain/computer. They are an intrinsic knowledge, present in the Centre, and linked to the original impulse towards separateness (see chapter 2).

As far as the Third-Eye Chakra is concerned, this is a latent ability derived from the Brain Chakra. In the Brain Chakra, this same latent ability appears as the capacity to invent things that are wholly new.

There is a centre in each of the Temples. The **Temple Chakras** are connected to the Eye Chakra and the Brain Chakra. They are also connected to the ears.

They are in fact terminals for receiving information similar to the way in which the ears register sound vibrations. It is the brain which interprets sound vibrations received from the material world of the four elements. Similarly, the Brain Chakra receives information via the Temple Chakra terminals from the fine material worlds and interprets it.

The development of these terminals paralleled that of the Third-Eye Chakra. The information they receive complements that received through the Third-Eye Chakra. This is why the Third-Eye Chakra and the Temple Chakras are connected both to each other and to the Brain Chakra from which they derive.

They are earlier than the ears, which came into existence as the mind pushed further out (and down) into matter.

Above the Brain Chakra is the **Crown Chakra**. This is located at the aperture of brahma where the two parietal bones meet (see Chart A).

This is the highest point of development achieved by the human form when the Centre pushes out and upwards to establish its "colonies in matter" (see page 43).

The form of this chakra can appear as an elongated sphere or an inverted, fully-opened lotus flower. The fully-opened lotus is at the upper end of the line of main chakras from the Base Chakra. The Base Chakra is the centre for the element Earth. The Sushumnā (see Chart A) is like the stalk of the lotus, rooted in earth from which its energy rises (see Kundalini).

The Buddha himself said:

"As a lotus flower is born in water, grows in water and rises out of water to stand above it unsoiled, so I, born in the world, raised in the world, having overcome the world, live unsoiled by the world."

The fact that it is inverted shows that at this point the evolving consciousness ceases to push further outward into matter in its search. It has exhausted the capabilities of the brain, all of which involve duality, and turns back and looks downwards for its origins.

At this point there is a realisation that the goal is not to find anything new, but to (re)discover where we came from and know it for the first time.

If the origin is perceived to be the Base Centre (and Kundalini), the wandering on will continue indefinitely. If it goes back further and deeper and finds the Centre, understanding dawns like sunrise and the journeying comes to an end.

There is a centre near the top of the head at the back. It is located at the aperture where the two parietal bones meet (and join) the occipital bone. This is the **Spirit Chakra**. Through this centre one becomes aware of a refined and pure consciousness, which acts as the guardian of an individual and makes possible contact with other beings. These beings are pure consciousness, content within their realm of being. This refined consciousness is the heaven of the "Pure Abodes".

There is a centre directly above the Brain Chakra, outside the head, about three inches above the top of the skull. It works like a transmitter. I have called it the **Brahmā Chakra.** (See next chapter).

There are centres below the Solar Plexus Chakra.

One is located in the centre of the body, above the sexual organ. It appears as a sphere of cloudy oatmeal colour and radiates desire. The **Desire Chakra** spins in association with the breathing. It expands with the inbreath and pushes out energy. It contracts with the outbreath and draws energy in. It has the feeling of water. It is primarily concerned with the urge for material survival and the reproduction of matter and material form.

Two to three inches below the Desire Chakra, is the **Base Chakra,** in front of the base of the spine. It has the feeling of earthiness. It radiates a pulsation like a drum or heartbeat. It is the opposite polarity to the Crown Centre (see Chart A).

Within it can be seen the mental image of a snake, its head resting on three coils, waiting to be awakened. This is **Kundalini**.

Particularly in India, it has been used (and still is) in an attempt to provide increased spiritual energy and realisation by "raising Kundalini". But since it activates the Desire Chakra during its ascent to the Crown Chakra, it becomes charged with sexual energy and the attempt usually results in long-term failure.

Although sexual energy can be refined and sublimated, it cannot transmute into spiritual energy.

Ascetics and yogis who attempt to transmute sexual energy fail because of a misconception about the basic natures of the subsidiary centres. Each of them has specific and therefore limiting characteristics. They derive *from* the Centre. They are therefore downstream of it. You cannot reach the source of a river by going downstream.

Ascetics who attempt to achieve permanent liberation in this way end up being trapped in sensual impulses and matter. They can be tracked down and investigated by anyone who cares to search for them (see chapters 12, 16).

All of these centres, with the exception of the Third-Eye Chakra, the Spirit Chakra and the Temple Chakras, are in a vertical line in front of the spine. They are linked by a fine channel of light, the sushumnā, in the centre of the spinal cord. Except for the Brahmā Chakra which is located outside the body.

The sushumnā does not pass through the chakras. The subsidiary centres branch off it like light bulbs (see Chart A, page 133).

There is also another channel of light which does pass through each chakra, including the Brahmā Chakra, and is linked to the Centre. I have called it the **Brahmā Channel** (see chapter 27).

Each centre generally gets its energy from the Centre through the Brahmā Channel. The flow is normally linked to the in and out breathing.

The energy in each centre can be intensified consciously by an act of will. It can also be intensified unconsciously or with partial consciousness as a response to the perception of sense objects.

Listening to Mozart, for instance, can lead to an intensification of awareness in the Brain Chakra and the Heart Chakra. The proximity of a female in season can produce intensification in the Desire Chakra. A perceived sense of danger can have a similar effect on the Throat Chakra. Music with a heavy drumbeat can stimulate the Base Chakra and, consequently, the Desire Chakra.

A perception of beauty can stimulate the Heart Chakra. However, if it is the beauty of *nature* that is perceived, one will notice that, after a while, the stimulation fades, as consciousness tends to subside towards the Centre itself.

As it subsides, the out-going energy flow from the Centre to the Heart Chakra diminishes.

The reason for this is that perception of the beauty of nature is usually accompanied by an awareness of its fundamental unity. This causes consciousness to home in spontaneously on the *source* of unity, the Centre itself.

The Brain Chakra is associated with images, memories and thoughts derived from or relating to sense objects at the sense doors.

Consequently, the flow of associative or consciously directed thinking can produce stimulation of any or all of the subsidiary centres. As can intellectual activities such as reading or watching films or even just conversation.

All of these examples of intensification of the energy flow from the Centre as an effect of sense contact can be overruled by an act of will or by consciously withdrawing one's attention from the sense doors to the Centre itself. This is of course an example of Upstreaming. (See chapter 22).

There are other, minor centres which are found in the arms and legs. I have included descriptions of these for completeness. It helps to build up a picture of how the astral body is constructed (see chapters 28 & 29) and how the relationship of mind and body works.

In chapter 24, it is explained how to enter the chakras. It is also possible to see that human consciousness can penetrate and *see* the functioning of even these "minor" chakras too.

The minor centres are: One in each **buttock**. One in each **groin**. One in each **knee**. One in each **ankle**. One in each

heel. One in the **ball of each foot**. The chakras of each pair are identical. They all derive their energy from the Centre via the Base Chakra.

In the **toes**, there are centres in the joints of each toe. In addition, there is a centre in the middle of the last segment of each toe.

There are similar pairs of centres in the arms: in the **shoulders**, the **elbows** and the **wrists**.

In the **hands**, there is a centre in the **palm** of each hand. There are centres in the joints of each **finger** (three in each, two in the thumb). In addition, there is a centre in the middle of the last segment of each finger.

In total, there is the original Centre plus 104 subsidiary centres. A total of 105 in all.

There are more details on all these subsidiary centres in chapter 24.

24. EXPLORING OTHER CENTRES

The subsidiary centres all have a location and usually emit a radiation and/or a vibration. The difference between radiation and vibration is really a matter of frequency. But from the point of view of actual *experience*, one can often *see* radiation when one cannot *feel* a vibration.

Some people can naturally locate these centres by *seeing* them. Some cannot see them and locate them by *feeling*. Those who can see them can usually feel them as well. Some can perceive (see or feel) only the more obvious ones.

Some can neither see nor feel any of them.

If one can't already see them, locating these centres will depend upon being able to feel the subtle and different vibrations that each emits. If one *can* feel them, one traces the feeling back to its point of origin. At this point one may be able to see them also.

Each of these centres is, in its own way, a gateway between the physical and non-physical planes of existence. Initially, what one sees or feels is the physical side of this gateway. One sees it from the point of view of the human being one has become now. The other side of the gateway are other worlds and planes of reality, where one has come *from* and where one may be reborn. These are accessed by actually *going through* the gateway(s).

But it is like the camel going through the eye of the needle. You can't take your material body with you into a purely mental universe.

Consequently, you find, if you do pass through, that you may have a different form. This will often resemble your present form. Finer or coarser, depending on whether you go to higher or lower levels of reality. Sometimes the form will be quite different. If you explore the world of aquatic creatures, you are likely to find that you look like a fish. On some levels, you will have no form at all. You will just be an observing consciousness.

METHOD USING THE SPHERE

One visualised a lighted sphere which made one visually aware of the Centre. This gives one the exact point where one had located the Centre. This activated the Centre. That is to say it made one visually aware of the Centre and gives one visual access to it. It also enables one to take advantage of some of the Centre's latent tendencies. For example, one can generate warmth, peace, relaxation and healing. (See chapter 18).

The sphere's size and intensity can be adjusted by the mind. It can also be moved to illuminate the inside of one's physical body and its brightness can be magnified so that the whole of the inside of the body is visible at the same time. When one moves the sphere, it is as though one were moving a lamp on a wandering lead which is connected to the mains. The sphere is the lamp. The wandering lead is the invisible connection between the Centre and the sphere and allows its latent powers to be applied where one wants them.

If one has developed the lighted sphere, it can be used to bring energy from the source Centre, which is upstream of the subsidiary centres, and *amplify* them so that their characteristics become visible for the first time. Or, if they were already visible, they will become more obvious.

One can also use the sphere to enable one to *enter* each centre and *experience* the level of reality to which it relates and is the gateway.

This is the same process as is used to explore the planes of reality opening out either side of the staircase. (See chapter 12).

Here, too, every time one enters a centre, one enters a world. In order to *be* there, one may acquire a form which has the senses required to contact that world. If one wants to experience the world of fishes, one may need a fish body. If one wants to experience eating one's way through the soil, one becomes an earthworm. And so on.

A lot of the difficulties which humans ordinarily experience in trying to understand levels of reality other than their own are due to the fact that, like scientists, they stay *outside* the level they are investigating.

Because of this, they acquire knowledge which is anchored in the observer's point of view. But knowledge acquired in this way often doesn't lead to an understanding or feeling of what it is like to *be* whatever it is that is being observed.

Ornithologists understand nothing of how birds feel and experience life, of what it is like to *be* a bird. Farmers understand nothing of farm animals and their feelings. Entomologists understand nothing of insects. Fishermen understand nothing of how a fish feels in the net or on the hook.

This is why they can kill (or cull) them.

Poets are different. A genuine poet has a highly specialised form of human awareness. Poets have a more or less tenuous awareness of the *oneness* or interconnectedness of nature and living beings. This leads to empathy. They can, in their imaginations, enter into the lives, the joys and sufferings of the beings around them.

Lovers can do this too but, unless they are also poets, they lose this ability when they stop loving.

PRACTICAL APPLICATION

In order to investigate the subsidiary centres, one moves the image of the lighted sphere from the Centre and positions it where one can *feel* or perhaps dimly perceive a subsidiary centre to be.

One uses the lighted sphere to activate each subsidiary centre in turn. Once one has done this a few times, one can go to each centre directly without needing to move the original sphere.

This is similar to using a candle to light other candles. Once they are alight (have been activated), they will be able to utilise the original fire themselves.

The sphere should be placed exactly where the centre is. In the case of these subsidiary centres, making it the size of a tennis ball or an orange is about right.

The colours of the various centres can vary. They are after all mental formations. There seem to be basic "default" colours, but the state of a being can affect the colours, as can moods and health. The more active and normal the functioning of a centre is, the brighter it appears. I have generally described "default settings".

One enters the spheres by *sinking* into them. This takes a little practice. But one cannot remain outside (the observer) and also *be* inside (the experiencer). It is similar to sinking into sleep except that one retains full consciousness of one's surroundings and self-awareness. It is possible to use the expansion method also (see page 56). Initially, it is better to sink into them.

The **Solar Plexus Chakra** is red. It is behind the solar plexus in the centre of the body. It is about the width of two fingers below the Centre. The radiation from it is of strength, power and confidence.

On entering this sphere, one may find that one has a male form, strong with a well-covered body; bare-chested, with ornaments on one's neck and upper arms. One's skin may be blue and one may be sitting on a blue lotus seat. One hears a buzzing like a swarm of bees. On the human level, one sees boxers fighting; on the animal level, lions, buffaloes, tigers fighting. One sees the ocean with great fish and sea creatures. On the heavenly planes are golden devas, talking, playing music, sitting peacefully. The demons (asuras) occupy themselves in displays of energy and strength such as tug-of-war.

The Solar Plexus Chakra is also the origin of the vital heat in the body. One can use the mind to turn up the heat from this centre just as one uses a dimmer switch to turn up the lights; warm > warmer > quite warm > very warm > hot > too hot > sweating.

At the present time, there are many ascetics whose practice in controlling the vital heat includes sitting on a large block of ice and melting it. Previously, there have been others who, wanting to make a spectacular exit, have induced what is now called 'spontaneous combustion'. For the rest of us, it's obvious that if one can control the vital heat, it will help in cold weather and act as an aid to good health.

If you find this hard to believe, consider that there is this latent reactive ability in your body to produce increased heat to combat the intrusion of disease. You get a high fever. The difference is that normally the onset of fever is *purely* reactive. In *using* the Solar Plexus Chakra, you take conscious control of the mechanism.

The energy drawn from the Centre via the Solar Plexus Centre can be increased, transmuted into strength and transmitted to other centres.

The **Heart Chakra** is seen to be smoky blue. It is in the middle of the chest and is easily located because of the many emotions that arise in association with it. It emanates a radiation, which is felt to have the qualities of goodwill: love, friendliness, sympathetic joy, compassion. (It also experiences the pain when these are thwarted).

At first this radiation seems to be confined within the physical frame. By making a mental determination, one can cause it to go beyond the body in all directions. The intensity can also be increased. If one does this, one will discover that other beings may perceive this (in their different ways) and respond accordingly.

The Heart Chakra operates on two levels: refined and unrefined. The unrefined level is more obviously dualistic. In this case, when one enters this sphere, one may discover that one has no form. However, since forms here are mind-made, one *can* take on whatever form, human, animal, deva, one considers appropriate just by making a mental intention to do so.

One perceives innumerable pairs of beings of different

kinds sharing blissful mutual affection. This is by no means always or exclusively physical. This is the level on which most humans experience this centre.

If one tries to communicate with these beings, one generally fails because each couple is totally absorbed in themselves, with no interest in or awareness of any other being.

This is a kind of unity in the sense that two halves joined together almost seem to re-establish the whole (see chapter 6).

Entering on the refined level, one takes on the form of a floating sphere or perhaps the four-faced form of Brahmā, each face emanating one of the four brahmavihāras; friendliness, sympathetic joy, compassion and equanimity.

On this refined level, one discovers, within the sphere, that there is a pervading scent of goodness and the occasional tinkling of a bell. What is seen is misty, blue space in which float spheres of different sizes and densities.

These spheres radiate the purest goodwill. It is not possible to make contact or communicate with these beings because each is complete in itself. Apart from the emanation of goodwill and the fact that they have refined forms that can be seen, one might have supposed that they had gone beyond duality altogether. The fact that they cannot be contacted shows that they almost have done. They have reached a stage where each is entirely satisfied within itself and has no need of, or curiosity about, any other whatsoever.

They are totally content to

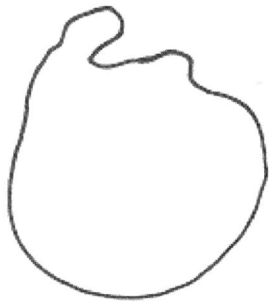

send out an uninterrupted stream of goodwill

Entering the Heart Chakra like this, one has gained access to one of the highest Brahmā worlds.

The differences in density and size of the spheres one sees reflect variations in the amount of good karma that each has accumulated.

Over time (exceedingly long time by our standards and reckoning), the spheres will gradually diminish and become more transparent until they fade away altogether.

The vanishing here is followed by an arising in another, lower level of existence (see chapter 12). There, previous karma in the form of latent tendencies will surface and they will resume their unending transmigration through the worlds until they are able to make an end of all this journeying on by realising Nibbāna.

The **Throat Chakra** is located behind the Adam's apple. The radiation from it is greenish blue and the feeling is of rivalry and competition. If one uses the sphere to enter it, one can hear the sound of lions roaring and fighting and dogs barking, the sound of metal clashing. One's form is similar to one's physical form, clothed in green and seated on white. There is nothing on the head except hair.

One sees innumerable battlefields with armies fighting and scenes of conflict. Rivalry and competition. Conquest and defeat. Winning and losing.

The **Brain Chakra** is in the middle of the head, in line with the space between the eyebrows. The sphere is golden and vibrating. When one uses the lighted sphere to enter it, one sees a dull greyness and hears a sound of buzzing like a swarm of bees. You can see millions of beings all busy inventing, making, painting, writing, thinking. There are hands with pens but without bodies.

You can meet Marie Curie. Her hair is combed back and gathered behind her neck. She is tired and pale. She is wearing a blue dress and an apron. She is holding a tube. At first, it seems that one cannot communicate with her. All these thinkers are in worlds of their own. The light in her Centre is very pale. It is possible, by using your mind, to make it brighter. This draws her attention away from her hands. In this way, you can make her see you.

> Would you like to rest?
> *Oh yes, I am tired.*
> Rest then.

You can make her Centre light even brighter until she smiles. When she smiles, she leaves her work and goes to a chair with a high back and arms. She sinks back into it with her feet on a footstool. She is now enjoying the fruit of her accumulated good karma until the restless wandering of speculative thought resumes.

The **Third-Eye Centre**. This is behind the space between the eyebrows and in line with the brain centre. From the outside it appears like a butterbean, either violet edged in gold, opaque in the centre, or dazzling white. It has two petals, like wings either side.

When one enters it, using the lighted sphere, one can sense a feeling of awe and hear a humming sound. Looking to see what form one appears in, one sees that one is an eye. In front of one is a kind of mandapa, a tall square pavilion with pillars and no walls. Gold and black. Empty.

It seems to be situated in space. Whatever (or whoever) you want to see, past, present or future, you make a mental intention for it/her/him to appear. If you have summoned up a person, you have no form by which they can see you. Although you can take one on if you choose. If you see a person, he will have a Centre visible in the centre of his body. You can deliberately make it brighter until he smiles, looks up and sees you. If it is someone whom you knew in the past, what will be visible to him is how you looked then, when you were last in physical contact with each other.

Ordinarily, he will assume that he is thinking about you or dreaming. If the experience is very vivid for him, he may think it is a ghost. Sometimes, communication is possible, just as if you were talking to each other in the presence of your bodies.

If it is someone who is dead, even someone quite close to you, or someone you have never met in the ordinary sense, you may find that they have little interest in you. You need to realise that they are seeing you in the context of where *they* are *now*. Any contact they may have had with you is likely to have faded significantly. Like a dream that was vivid when you woke up but, by mid-morning, can hardly be remembered at all. You can generally, though, question them as to how they reached their present level of being and what things they did previously that led to this. They may have no interest in you but they will not yet have lost interest in themselves.

Always, one can benefit these beings to some extent by mentally intensifying the light in their Centres up to the point when they smile. The smile is an indication that, at that moment at least, they are happy. Then you can mentally let them go and they will fade away and vanish from you.

The **Temples Chakras** have spheres that are a clear, dark blue. They are seen to be contracting and expanding and emitting waves of energy. On entry, one sees that one has a light blue female form sitting on a darker blue lotus. One sees groups of people sitting around a table of food. Two reach out at the same time for the same dish. There are people standing under a fruit tree. Two reach for the same fruit at the same time. There is a vision of an ancient Burmese army advancing towards a river. Naresuan, the opposing Thai king, *senses* their approach before they can be seen and moves to meet them at the same time.

These two centres operate by what would be called extrasensory perception. They perceive events and beings either on another plane altogether or on the same plane but out of range of the five senses.

There is a centre at the top of the head above the brain centre. This is the **Crown Chakra**. It is located at the aperture of brahma where the two parietal bones meet. In appearance it is like an upside-down lotus flower, golden and grey with innumerable petals, about six inches across. It can also be seen as an elongated sphere which follows the contour of the skull.

When one enters it, the feeling is a concentrated radiation of bliss, peace and silence. One's form is that of a small black-haired boy with topknot and golden skin, seated on a white lotus with pink tips to its petals. Spheres can be seen forming and instantly disappearing again. There are no sounds.

The baby boy is Buddha, the fully awakened human consciousness. The lotus faces downwards. This indicates that, from this point, all efforts are to be directed to the perfection of human beings and their enlightenment, rather than towards continued upward development to rival the state of the gods.

There is a centre at the back of the top of the head. This is the **Spirit Chakra**. It is located where the two parietal bones meet and join the occipital bone. There is a whorl of hair (very rarely two) at this point on the surface of the skull.

The sphere is clear, dark violet like lavender. It radiates peace and mellow, positive feelings. Entering the sphere, one has no form, just consciousness. One sees space, which is violet: peaceful, misty and opaque. Music is heard played by string instruments and one can see musicians, with black hair and thin garments around their waists.

Consciousness can exit the body through this aperture. This accesses a level on which the beings are of pure consciousness, solitary and content within their fields. It is "The Pure Abodes" and is reached by meditating on Peace. This purifies the mind.

There is a Guardian Deity named Suti, who has been here for millions of years already and will remain here "for many more kalpas".

> Can Nibbāna be reached from this world?
> *Yes, if one is a non-returner before one dies.*

Suti is not a non-returner.

The **Brahmā Chakra** is located outside the body three inches above the head in line with the Brain Chakra. It can appear as a yellow or radiant blue full moon. It radiates courage, purity and peace in all directions. When one enters it by means of the sphere, one may find that one has a form, transparent but without a Centre. This indicates that at that time, one has no attachment to any separateness or becoming and is in a plane of reality that corresponds to this state.

One may be seated on a white or transparent lotus. There is an intermittent high humming sound. In front is clear space with a background that seems blue because of its immensity. One looks to see where the radiation of peace one perceives emanating from this centre is coming from. One discovers it is coming from oneself. In this chakra one is simply transmitting peace in all directions indiscriminately. Continuously.

In this state, one realises that the humming sound is in fact the continuous chanting of OM. Looking to see where it is coming from, one finds that it is coming both from within oneself and also outside.

One can see an enormous hall in the form of a cave, the walls of which are without windows and shining. It is full of people, dressed in the same white loose robes, sitting in rows and meditating. Most have long beards and hair. Some sit on tiger skins. Some on mats. It is they who are chanting OM.

They are facing a very old Brahmin sitting on a tiger skin. His eyes are nearly black. You can make him aware of you and communicate with you. This level is called *Santi,* the Holy Place. This Brahmin has been here for 500 years.

> Is healing possible from here?
> *Yes, if the disease is not too chronic.*
> How?
> *From this state of peace and holiness, direct the mind towards the suffering.*
> Is it possible to reach Nibbāna from here?
> *Yes.*

The Brahmin says his duty is to continue vibrating OM to the world until his time here is up.

The sphere can be made to move away, with one in it, independent of the physical body.

From it can be seen the astral bodies of others encased in their physical bodies. Often, the astral body appears as the younger version of the physical body. Sometimes, it has the appearance of the body of the previous birth; a bearded man inside a female physical body, for example. If the previous birth had been an animal, that is how the astral form may appear.

Occasionally, where the physical body has been "possessed" by an alien spirit, this is what can appear. It is possible for more than one alien spirit to inhabit the same physical and, if so, that is what will be seen.

If, while one is in this centre, one allows one's mind to become completely tranquil, one acquires the form of the Great Brahmā with four faces and many arms. One's colour is greeny-blue. One has a gold headpiece, pointed at the centre. One hears nothing. One feels nothing. But one is able to see anything one wishes, or any person, with a single thought.

There are also chakras in the lower part of the body.

Below the Solar Plexus Chakra, the **Desire Chakra** is located just above the sexual organ. When latent, it is oatmeal colour, becoming red as it is activated. Entering the sphere, one may find a female form, dressed in red, sitting on a blue lotus. The sphere is spinning in phase with the breathing. It contracts on breathing in and expands on pushing out. One sees innumerable babies, human and animal, together with pregnant females and mating couples. There is also a feeling of desire to be free from all this.

About two inches below this is the **Base Chakra**. The feeling is earthiness. Entering the pale yellow sphere, one's form is a large green, brown and yellow snake with red eyes. Coiled. There is a sound of continuous pulsation and a feeling of yearning. In front of one is a large golden sphere. This is the Crown Chakra! The snake, you, is yearning to be united with the Crown Chakra.

The main centres are linked to a fine line of light which can be intensified (see Chart A). It goes from the Base Chakra to the Crown Chakra. At the Brain Chakra, there are branches off to the Third-Eye Chakra, the Spirit Chakra and the Temple Chakras. This straight line is the **Sushumnā** (see chapter 27). It lies in the middle of the spinal cord nerve. All the main centres, except the Brahmā Chakra, are connected to the Sushumnā. The Centre itself is *not* connected to the Sushumnā.

There is *another* channel which links all these main subsidiary centres to the Centre called the **Brahmā Channel** (see chapter 27). This connection actually goes through them, though the Centre can by-pass any of them if required. (Actually because the Centre is fundamentally non-physical it can act with or independently of any physical or astral component of the individual being!) This channel passes through and above the Crown Chakra and reaches the external Brahmā Chakra.

There are centres below the Base Chakra down to the toes. It is possible to visualise these as spheres too and enter them. Ordinarily, they do not contain any observing consciousness but function automatically like the parts of a living machine. When one does enter them one is able to observe a visualization of the activities that they make possible.

There are centres in the **Groins**. The spheres are pale yellow, opaque and not spinning. There is a throbbing vibration from them, a feeling of flexibility. On entering them, one finds that one has no form, just consciousness. One sees beings endlessly getting up and down.

In the **Buttocks**, the centres are violet and spinning. Entering, one senses a feeling of stability. One has no form. One sees beings sitting on the ground. Mostly cross-legged; sometimes with their knees bent and their legs drawn up under them.

The **Knee** Chakras are opaque violet blue; the form is that of a human dressed in white, seated on a white lotus. The feeling is of 'being in motion'. Everywhere can be seen beings running; horses, other animals, humans.

The **Ankle** Chakras are transparent, golden brown and spinning. One's form is human, dressed in orange on a brown lotus. One sees feet, hoofs and paws running and jumping. They are attached to bodies, but it is the feet themselves that stand out.

The **Heel** Chakra spheres are brown and static. When one enters them, one finds one's form is human. The feeling is of steadiness and stability. One sees a landscape of roots.

The **Balls** of the feet have dull, white spheres and are quite stable without any radiation. One is formless. One sees beings dancing and spinning and jumping.

In the **Toes**, there are centres in the joints of each toe (three in each, two in the big toe). In addition, there is a centre in the middle of the last segment of each toe.

The joint at the base of the big Toe has a centre that is brown and vibrating. When one enters this, there is no sound and one has no form. The feeling is a mixture of stability and security. The big toe is an extension of the foot. When one walks (without shoes) one secures each step using the big toes. One sees images of many different kinds of feet moving.

The next joint is the "operator". The centre is a lighter brown and vibrating. On entering one has no form. One hears clicking sounds. The feeling is as with the lower joint but more active. One sees feet firm on the ground without slipping.

The sphere in the top centre of the toe is an even lighter brown and vibrating. The feeling is more active and agile. One sees old people from earlier generations or natives who had never worn shoes. Their big toes are prominent and bent like hooks to secure each step and prevent slipping in wet and slippery ground.

The centres of the other toes are yellow but are seen to have similar characteristics, strengthening and supporting the function of the big toes, when one enters them. In every case, although one has consciousness and can perceive quite clearly, one has no form.

All these centres derive their energy and livingness through the Base Chakra.

There is also a flow of energy to and from the earth via these centres.

In the soles of the feet one can see many luminous "threads" leading up to the Solar Plexus Chakra. Then there is a link from the Solar Plexus Chakra to the Centre, two finger-breadths above it. There are also threads leading to the other main centres and, via them, to physical organs.

The thread from the foot to the Base Centre is an opaque white. Some of the others are clear, some are not. The thickest is the one from the foot to the physical heart via the solar plexus and from the physical heart to the Centre.

There is a grey thread from the foot to the small intestine. When squeezed, it becomes brighter. When energy from the Centre is pumped to the small intestine, the thread becomes brighter and the other end of the string in the foot tingles.

The reason for these links between the organs and the feet is survival. As the (bare) foot touches the earth, it absorbs energy from the earth and receives a natural massage and toning for the organ. Feet are similar to roots. They can absorb energy food and sense the nature of the terrain.

There are centres in the arms. They are linked to each other and the Shoulder Chakras and these are linked to the Heart Chakra. Using the lighted sphere from the Centre to amplify them changes their size and sometimes colour.

The **Shoulder** Chakras have blue revolving spheres radiating a feeling of mobility. If one uses the lighted sphere, the chakras appear light gold. The feeling is of firmness. Entering, one has no form and hears no sound. One sees men and women wielding swords and tennis rackets and similar images.

The **Elbow** Chakras have brown/green spheres. They are radiating but not spinning. There is no form or sound and one sees people doing exercises.

The **Wrist** Chakras have blue spheres radiating and spinning. One hears a clattering sound. One sees Buddha images, some with hands raised, some with one hand on knee. There are images of people using their hands in innumerable ways.

There is a centre in the **Palm** of each hand. It is golden. Entering it, one has no form. People can be seen shaking hands in friendship or using their hands for healing. Although most people shake hands more or less automatically, a handshake is actually the medium for the transference of positive energy between individuals. If you are fully aware when you do it, you can easily feel this. You can also sense immediately if someone is not in contact with you and withholding his friendship (or even worse).

The fingers have centres in each joint and also in the last segment (the one with the nail).

The **Thumb** has a yellow/gold, vibrating sphere in the base joint. Entering it, one finds one has consciousness but no form and there are no sounds. This is true with the other centres in the thumb also. One sees hands picking things up and putting them down and people using their thumb(s) as a means of communication.

The joint halfway up the thumb has a blue vibrating sphere. Entering the sphere, one sees hands gripping objects.

The last segment has a yellow vibrating sphere. Entering it, one senses that this emits a vibration of power and firmness; one sees men gripping a thick rope.

When one enters the centres in the fingers, one has consciousness but no form and, usually, there are no sounds to be heard.

The **Index Finger**. In the first joint, the centre has a red sphere vibrating a sense of authority. One sees kings and rulers pointing with this finger while giving orders to those who are below them.

The centre in the second joint has a pink vibrating sphere and radiates a feeling of confidence and authority. There is a sound of clattering and soldiers are to be seen pulling triggers.

Entering the third joint centre, one also sees soldiers pulling the triggers of guns.

The centre in the last segment of this finger also radiates authority. One sees fingers pointing. If they are pointed with good feelings, they produce happiness. Bad feelings cause discomfort, pain or, if the negative feeling has great intensity, death.

The **Middle Finger** links to the stomach. The sphere in the joint at the base of the finger is blue and vibrating. Entering it one has no form but there is a continuous whirring sound in the background and a feeling of cooperation with the thumb. One sees a high mountain and the middle finger represents the peak of this. This peak provides a stabilising post for things. One can see golden devas on the mountain with headpieces and bare arms, neck decorations and ornate belts. One can feel a flow of energy being transmitted from the earth into the hand and vice versa.

The second joint up has a centre that is light blue. The vibration produces a feeling of agility. There is no form but the same sound can be heard as in the previous one. The middle part of a high mountain can be seen with female devas.

The third joint has a misty light blue centre. Entering it, there is no form or sound. Feelings and what is seen are the same as the previous centre but to a lesser degree.

The top segment of the finger has a sphere, which is grey, white and vibrating. There is no form or sound and the feeling is one of openness, similar to when you are on top of a mountain. A figure is seen, holding a torch, similar to the Statue of Liberty. The colour is bronze and the dazzling white radiation from the torch seems to be coming from the tip of the finger. If you touch the earth with this finger while investigating this centre, you can feel energy flowing through it all the way from the earth to the Centre and vice versa. (Compare the soles of the feet, page 127).

The centre in the base of the **Ring Finger** has a vibrating gold sphere. When one enters it one has no form. A shrill whistling sound can be heard. There is a feeling of friendliness. One sees a man putting a ring on a woman's finger.

The joint above has a pale gold centre. In it there is no form and no sound. It radiates a feeling of agreement and seems to be a symbol of agreement and contact between pairs of human beings.

The joint above has a yellow centre. In it there is no form or sound. It is subordinate to and supportive of the previous centre. One sees groups working together, families, both human and animal.

The centre in the tip of the finger is amber. In it there is no form or sound. One sees people living in concord, couples that get on well. The feeling is supportive.

The **Little Finger's** lowest centre is purple and vibrating. There is no form or sound. The feeling is of people coming together after discord. Reconciliation. What is seen are shaking hands, smiling, animals rubbing their bodies against each other. Couples walking with their little fingers linked.

The next centre is pale blue but similar to the previous one.

The third is paler blue but otherwise the same.

In the top of the finger, the feeling in the centre is forgiveness. The centre is violet. People and animals are seen sitting together, eating and drinking together.

Branching out from the subsidiary centres are what yogis call *nadis*. "Nadis" (the Sanskrit for "tubes" or "pipes") are channels through which, in traditional Indian medicine and spiritual science, the energy from the Centre flows through the astral body.

The chakras, sushumnā, and the web of nadis form the structure of the astral body, which superimposes upon and interpenetrates the matter of the physical body and creates its duplicate in the molecular physical structure.

In the physical, it appears as the chemical-electrical central nervous system with its network of nerves.

While it is superimposed, the physical is full of livingness. When it withdraws, it leaves a physical copy which functions for a while as a material machine before decaying and disintegrating.

One might compare it to an electrical circuit. While the current is turned on, all the various appliances function properly. The moment it is turned off and their source of energy disappears, they stop working.

The physical has an overall coherent appearance such that, with our fleshy eyes, we don't just see molecules, chemicals, bones and nerves but a recognisable man or woman with individual characteristics.

Similarly, with our astral vision, we don't just see chakras, sushumnā and nadis, but a recognisable astral being, young or old, male or female. This can be human, deva, or even animal. (See chapter 28).

25. CHART A

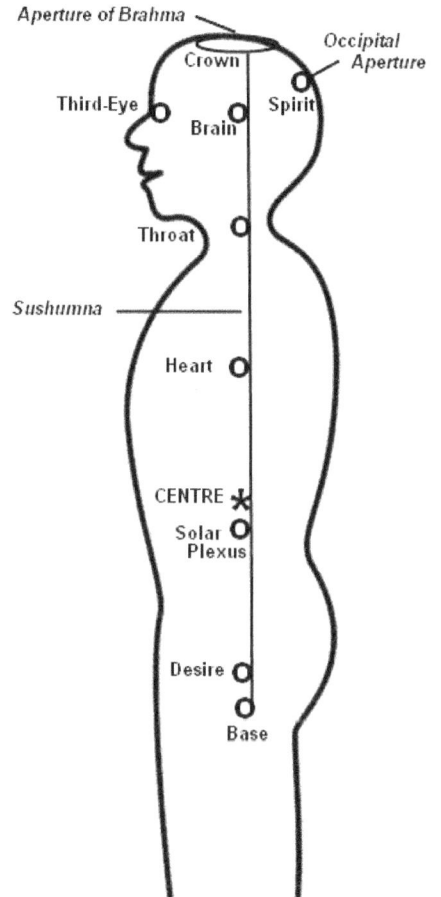

**SUSHUMNĀ AND MAIN CHAKRAS
WITHIN THE HUMAN BODY**

26. CHART B

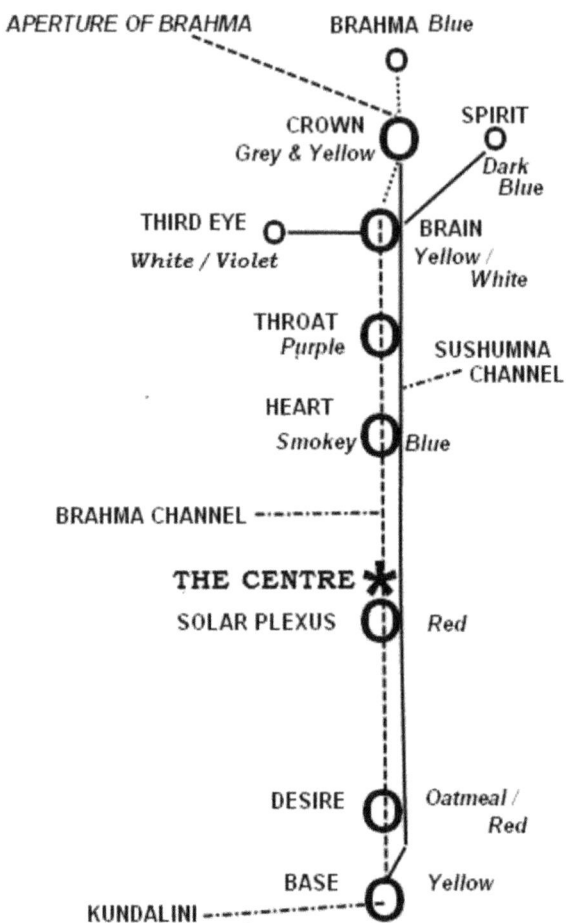

MAIN CHAKRAS & CHANNELS

27. THE THREE CHANNELS

There are three "central" or "median" channels. The "physical", the "astral" and the "brahmā" channel.

The *physical* channel is the *spinal* cord, enclosed within the spinal cavity and forming part of the central nervous system. On a physical level, nerves sense your external and internal surroundings and communicate information between your brain and spinal cord. Nerves carry electrochemical signals to and from different areas of the nervous system as well as between the nervous system and other tissues and organs.

The *astral* channel is the *sushumnā*. It is a quarter of an inch wide and is located exactly in the middle of the spine. It links the centres from the Base Chakra to the Crown Chakra. It is golden. It stops at the Crown Chakra. This is why, ordinarily, those who raise Kundalini are unable to perceive the Brahmā Chakra, which is *outside the body* and above the head. The Third-Eye and Spirit Chakras branch off from the Brain Chakra. So do the Temple Chakras.

The sushumnā enables energy from the Centre to flow from chakra to chakra and through the nadis which branch out like veins of golden light. These provide livingness to the nerves of the physical body.

When the astral body leaves the physical body, sushumnā goes with the astral body. As do the centres. The physical structure with its central nervous system is left behind. As is Kundalini.

The Centre is not linked to the sushumnā.

The *brahmā* channel links the Centre to the subsidiary centres, independently of the sushumnā. It is golden. It is just over two inches in front of the sushumnā and parallel to it. It is a little narrower than the sushumnā. It passes out through the Crown Chakra and the aperture of brahma to the Brahmā Chakra where it opens out and disappears into the universe. The other end of this line enters the Base Chakra, then divides, and passes down the legs and into the feet; there, if uninhibited, to make contact with the earth.

When the brahmā form withdraws and leaves the astral form, the sushumnā disappears into the Centre from which it originally appeared during the journey outwards towards the creation of matter. The subsidiary centres also disappear. In fact, both the sushumnā and the centres developed *out of* the Centre via the brahmā channel during the course of outward evolution.

28. ASTRALS AND ASTRAL TRAVEL

An astral is a type of disembodied spirit, that is, a being which is not composed of gross matter. Matter is the substance of which all physical objects consist: typically, molecules, atoms and subatomic particles.

"*Astral travel*" is a term used when providing an interpretation of one form of out-of-body experience. It assumes the existence of an "astral body" separate from the physical body and capable of travelling outside it. Astral projection or travel denotes the astral body leaving the physical body to travel in the astral plane.

In an out-of-body experience, the spiritual traveller leaves the physical body and travels in his subtle or dream body or astral body into "higher realms". It is therefore associated with near-death experiences and is also frequently reported as spontaneously experienced in association with sleep and dreams, illness, surgical operations, drug experiences, paralysis and forms of meditation.

It may involve "travel to higher realms" called astral planes but is commonly used to describe any sensation of being "out of the body" in the everyday world, even seeing one's body from outside or above.

The fact is that astrals certainly exist.

Inside every living body, there is an astral body. Usually, its form is a younger version of the physical. It can, however, be the form of the previous birth and can therefore appear as an animal (including snakes) or a deva (angel) or even a demon. It is not necessarily the same sex as the physical, which accounts for one form of homosexuality.

However, astrals do not have gross physical sexual organs like penises and vaginas. These are strictly related to reproduction and involve some degree of awakening of Kundalini, which is latent in the Base Centre. The sexual differences in astrals (and devas) are obvious but far more refined.

When the astral body is in the physical, both astral and physical are operative. Therefore, sexual attraction can be wholly astral, wholly physical or (usually) a mixture of the two in variable proportions.

The astral body energises the physical body using energy from the Centre via the centres. When the astral leaves the physical body, the body is "empty". No sushumnā, no centres, no nadis. Just physical organs which continue to function like a machine. Kundalini stays with the physical body, in the perineum, latent.

The astral can leave the physical body consciously through the aperture of brahma, the occipital aperture, the Centre and straight out through the front of the body (rather like stepping out of a wardrobe). It can also leave without full consciousness as in sleep. It can move around the room, pass through walls, fly out of the window et cetera.

The astral takes with it the energy output of the Centre to the centres and nadis and can *feel* this, even without a physical form.

Astrals are found on the astral plane, when someone has temporarily left his body. They are also found when the body is dead and the astral remains and has not moved on to a new birth. In this case, the astral is a type of ghost. Not all ghosts are astrals however.

An astral has a set of five astral senses, including an astral eye with which it can see the astral plane. This is identical with the "third" eye. It can also see other astrals including the astral bodies inside living human bodies.

The astral plane is a mental plane of being. It can also contain remembered images of the physical plane (including memories of pictures), imagined scenes and also representations of a physical scene located on the time-track (i.e. that is what it looked like *then*, now it may be quite different). For this reason, astrals often go back to old haunts and find them unfamiliar. The cottage they grew up in may now be a factory car park.

Astrals can enter other bodies even if the other astral is already there. Astrals can also see the astrals in other bodies. But they have difficulty in seeing the physical bodies themselves. Physical eyes are usually needed to see the physical plane.

Sometimes both the physical eye and astral eye are active in a person at the same time, especially at night, fading light or during strong emotion such as fear or excitement. This is why it is possible for one man to see a "ghost" but not the man standing next to him. In one, the astral eye is active at that time, in the other it is not.

The astral eye finds it very difficult to see the physical plane as it actually is in the present. This is why when one sees a ghost, it often does not see one and may in fact pass right through one. Invariably, if this happens, one feels a chill. There is no heat in astrals and no heat on the astral plane.

Babies and very young children often, without realising it, use both astral and physical eyes at the same time. This is why a baby will lie on its back and smile and laugh and gurgle while looking at the ceiling or an unoccupied corner of the room. Often it is communicating with another astral that it recognises, especially if it has been reborn in the same house where it had been an astral before its conception. Usually the parents are unaware that this is happening.

More seriously, if there is a malignant astral in the house, the baby may become frightened and cry for its mother (the only point of safety it knows apart from the Centre). Again the parents will not be able to understand it. Nor will doctors or nurses. Once its "exteriorisation" progresses, this will pass. Although it will tend to recur when the child is left alone.

There is an oddity. Most of those who can see in the astral plane are surprised at how *few* astrals are to be seen. Whereas those who see on the physical plane are aware of just how thickly populated our planet is.

Partly this is because when beings die, they mostly move on almost immediately to the next birth, driven on by the momentum of karma.

There is another reason. On the physical plane, generally one sees anything which comes within one's field of being. If you don't want to see it, either you close your eyes or look away, thereby removing it from your field of vision.

On the mental plane, everything is already there. But you need to *look* for it with your astral eye. You need to *intend* to see. The exception to this is when a mental body *intends* you to see it. Perhaps it is coming to claim some karmic debt or wants to terrify you. Or perhaps because it likes you and wants to communicate.

So the next time you are on the astral plane and are surprised that there is no one else there, *intend*. Think, "Let something or someone appear!" Something or someone will.

Astrals have astral eyes (the third-eye), astral ears, a sense of smell and taste, feeling and consciousness. When the astral is in the physical, one or more of these may be active intermittently.

So a human may think that what he sees is really there physically.

Or again, using the astral ear unwittingly, the human may "hear" things, voices or objects being moved or unusual sounds; but when he looks to see what is happening, there is nothing to be seen. Others, who may be around, have heard nothing untoward.

Furthermore, the astral can feel. So a man can suddenly feel cold, disturbed, or afraid, but when he looks, there is nothing there to cause the feeling. There is, of course. But it is not physical; it is on the astral plane.

"Astral" comes from Greek άστρον (astron) "star". Before Galileo's telescope, astral travelling was supposed to occur on a plane of existence that included heaven, hell and the heavenly bodies (stars). When telescopes failed to reveal anything other than obviously material planets and suns, astral travel became more accurately defined as a mental phenomenon.

However, these astral forms, which, being mental, are unaffected by physical obstructions, are impervious to heat and cold and can travel at any speed they wish, can be used to explore outer space and its contents without the limitations and expense of space ships.

Because of the existence of the time track, it is possible to travel to a planet and track it back to its origin. This is actually best done while one is alive and in contact with one's physical body. The brain is a useful tool for evaluating the data.

But there is another reason for doing it while one is still alive. When one loses one's physical body, it is very difficult to summon up any interest in things like "the origin of the solar system" and "was there life on Mars?"

As any schoolboy knows, in the total absence of interest or desire, concentration is almost impossible. Without concentration, sustained mental effort cannot occur.

29. ASTRALS, DEVAS AND BRAHMĀS

There are astrals that can be encountered outside of physical bodies. They have forms which often resemble those of their previous births. They are generally *between* births. They can remain for a very long time; often in the same location, occasionally wandering on.

Usually, they are solitary and do not interact with each other, although it is possible to come across them in groups; sometimes there are whole armies where there has been a battle, all encapsulated in a common emotional field.

Astrals are not limited to human forms. There are also astrals of animals, including snakes. There is an astral adder that inhabits a pampas clump in my garden.

The state of an astral is not one in which it is normally possible to make any kind of progress. Astrals have no obvious needs. They do not require material food. Although they can remember things if questioned, they seem to exist out of time; sitting, watching - yet not waiting; with no awareness of time's passing. If there is a strong mental imprint from the past, they will repeat, over and over again, the same activities; shipwrecked sailors in a sunken ship tinkering in the engine room or cleaning decks. They will pace up and down or lie on a couch or sit in a chair.

They have Centres although they are not aware of them unless this is pointed out to them. The colours vary. They do not know what they are but they can enter them, if told to, and they experience a greater sense of peace.

They are aware of the humans that share a location with them. But they usually show no particular interest in them. If a human does catch their interest, they may follow it about rather as a dog does.

However, if an opportunity presents itself to enter a womb – they see a mating couple – the desire to be reborn may arise and they will take it. It therefore happens that, in an old house, an astral can be born again into the same family that he previously died in: the grandfather can become his grandson, for example. He could also be reborn as the dog!

This kind of thing was common in times and places in which there was little change for long periods of time; particularly where people died and were born in the same house, rather than in nursing homes and hospitals.

So, in a village or small community, a group of beings could come and go, inter-relating, changing roles and becoming the prisoners of the karma they created among themselves; their feuds and loves. This is much less common in the modern westernised world, where beings wander off over wider areas (although still taking with them the imprints of former feuds and loves which germinate if they ever do meet and may, if they are serious enough, actually draw them together).

Devas, too, are disembodied beings. They differ from astrals in that they are not between births. They have already been reborn in accordance with their karma. The requirement for rebirth as a deva is generosity and morality. Some of them may also have developed meditation. They get on with the business of their new state. They interact with other devas.

Deva in its more limited sense refers to beings in the six

planes immediately above the human one, the sensuous heavens. They can live for hundreds or thousands of years.

The devas of the sensuous sphere enjoy sense pleasures in far greater abundance than can be found in the human world. Their bodies emit light and they have subtle sense organs, similar to ours but far more powerful and acute.

It is worthwhile emphasising that in the process of outward development from the Centre, the subtle non-physical sense organs came *before* copies of those organs appeared simultaneously with matter as it evolved in order to contact it.

Devas are generally happy because they are free from the burdens and problems of a human body. Some of their perceived needs and desires are met by making mental intentions. "Let such and such appear!" Others are inherited from the efforts they made previously on the human plane. They do show some interest in the affairs of men since, in many cases, they were men and women in former births.

"Devas" is a broad term. It covers beings of mental construction - gods (but not brahmās), angels, guardian angels and household gods (what the Roman world called lares and penates). The gods and angels inhabit specific heaven worlds, though they are not confined there. The household gods remain in a particular dwelling.

Other devas include beings which move around quite freely in the parallel worlds of astral and material form. They inhabit trees, plants, streams, rivers and even flowers. Most of the English names familiar to us for this kind of deva derive from Graeco-Roman culture: *Naiads*, nymphs of fountains, wells, springs, streams and brooks; *Dryads*, the nymphs of trees; *Anthoussai*, nymphs of flowers.

In Buddhist southeast Asia, if a deva has been seen living in a particular tree, you will see a large, red, green or yellow muslin-type cloth wrapped around the trunk, which indicates that it should not be cut down. Offerings are made to it (the deva), such as lighted joss sticks, rice and fruit.

When the trees and bushes in which these devas live are destroyed, the devas are not destroyed, any more than the astral is killed when its physical body dies. They simply lose their homes, just as human beings do if their houses burn down and they escape the fire.

However, they can and do experience loss and sorrow and may therefore fade away ("die").

They can also experience anger. This may result in hostile actions aimed at those responsible. Of course, they cannot normally impinge upon the physical human form directly. But they can reach the mind. They can implant self-destructive thoughts. (How many of those accused in the courts of crimes blame it on voices?) They can cause dreams and nightmares.

On the higher deva planes are also found what Buddhism calls "stream-enterers" and "once-returners".

There are also bad spirits, which are not called devas but asuras (denizens of darkness) – demons and devils in our culture. These do actually have a considerable ability to act in a hostile way to humans. They are the mental equivalents of poisonous insects and snakes. Just as the insects and snakes transmute their food into physical poisons that damage the human body, so the asuras transmute their mental "food" or energy into mental poisons that can damage the human mind.

When materialism was at its height, this way of looking at things became unfashionable. The symptoms of intrusion into the human mind by hostile beings still occurred in humans, but different materialistic causes had to be found, such as chemicals or genetic weaknesses. Now, as the comprehensive materialistic view of life loses its attraction, the older, universal way of looking at these things is returning.

Brahmās, too, are disembodied beings. They are more highly developed than astrals or devas. To be born as a brahmā requires not only generosity and morality (as for devas), but also mental development through meditation.

Brahmās with forms have extremely subtle bodies of light; their powers are great but not unlimited. A being is reborn among these brahmās by cultivating the appropriate level of meditation (jhāna), perfecting it, and retaining it at the moment of death. Jhānas are states of deep concentration that can be attained by unifying the mind through meditation. They are all wholesome states of a very lofty and sublime nature.

The beings in the brahmā planes spend most of their time enjoying their respective jhānas. Brahmās experience no ill will or hatred, but only because they have suppressed it by their jhāna, not because they have uprooted it from their mental continuum. Thus, when a brahmā is eventually reborn as a deva or human being, he or she can again be affected by hatred.

It can even happen that, after rebirth as a deva or human, a former brahmā can fall to one of the lower planes of suffering, the hell worlds. This would be because of the ripening of an unwholesome karmic seed from an earlier birth.

The brahmās are also prone to conceit and belief in a permanent self (see page 17), as well as to attachment to the bliss of meditation.

Brahmās can interact with the human plane if they so choose, but to appear to humans they must, like the devas, deliberately assume a grosser form, unless the humans have activated their Third-Eye Chakras.

All of these beings, astrals, devas, asuras and lower brahmās are beings made of mind. They are sometimes said to be made of refined matter, but since there is no material substance in them which can be perceived or measured by material instruments, this is a misnomer. It is better to see them as having a non-physical *form* (similar to an image in a mirror), with progressively refined senses and consciousness.

They can be seen by the astral, deva or brahmā eye, just as physical forms can be seen by physical eyes.

There is another, higher class of brahmās. These are the formless brahmās. They have no subtle bodies of light and no refined mental senses. They consist entirely of pure mind. They attained this kind of birth by developing and maintaining the formless jhānas. These are four kinds of absorption which take abstract formless concepts as objects; the dimension of infinite space, the dimension of infinite consciousness, the dimension of nothingness, the dimension of neither perception nor non-perception. The karmic result of doing this becomes operative at their death.

These brahmās can have no contact with the human or deva planes; for they have no bodies of form and there is nothing that can be seen.

They spend unimaginably long periods of time in the perfect equanimity of meditation until their lifespan ends, i.e. the karmic energy (merit) that sustains them runs out. Then they are reborn in a lower plane or as devas. The Buddha's former teachers are probably here.

After that they too can be reborn on any plane at all as a result of some previous karmic action. So even existence without the subtlest kind of form (see page 16) is not the way to permanently eliminate suffering.

There is another kind of disembodied being which is of great interest. It is not an astral because it does not, normally, contain the sushumnā, nor the subsidiary centres. "Deva" does not fit its state of development. While "brahmās" are a bit too remote.

In many parts of the world, there are Buddha images, religious icons, holy relics and places where, it is believed, the saintly (or demonic) individual associated with them lingers on. Prayers and offerings and sacrifices are made to these. Healing often occurs, prayers are sometimes answered and visions appear to some.

In the modern world, such places become great commercial centres attracting tens of thousands of pilgrims. Canterbury in the Middle Ages and Lourdes are famous examples in the west.

In the east, in Chachoengsao, the Temple of Luang Por Sothorn is another. *Luang Por* literally means "Venerable Father". It is also a term of respect for a senior monk. *Sothorn* is the name of an old temple. It comes from *Sao Tong*, meaning "flag pole".

So great has been the growing faith in Luang Por Sothorn that, a generation ago, Chachoengsao was a provincial town with a small plastered brick temple. Now it is a large and prosperous, increasingly commercialised town. In it is a complex centred around an enormous temple which has been financed by the voluntary donations of the faithful. This temple is one of the most magnificent in southeast Asia. It is a wonderful synthesis of faith, money, architectural brilliance and supreme technical skill.

Despite the growing upsurge of factories and industrial units, the economy of Chachoengsao still depends for much of its increasing prosperity on the thousands of pilgrims who flock here like seagulls to a fish factory, to be healed in mind and body and have their prayers for winning lottery tickets and the fertility of their wives granted. (And spend their money on food, souvenirs and hotels).

Inside this temple is a famous Buddha image which is supposed to have floated here on the Bang Pakong River after the destruction of Ayudhya by the Burmese in 1767.

The faith of the faithful *needs* to be strong for the bronze image cannot actually be seen. Because of its growing reputation as a granter of prayers and its small size, there was fear that it might be stolen. So it is said it was hidden inside a large plaster statue of Buddha.

This plaster Buddha has a twisted lip and hides within it an older dark-bronze image, twelve inches high. This does not have a twisted lip and is of late Ayudhya period, with a high-pointed head covering. It is hidden to deter thieves and guarded by five Devas. Their chief, Sutee, has a moustache.

There is a more visible guard of armed policemen.

The faithful believe that inside the image itself is the spirit of Luang Por Sothorn, a famous monk, who after the fall of Ayudhya, is believed to have rejected Nibbāna and entered this bronze Buddha image for the benefit of others. Amulets with his image have sold for up to 40,000 baht each.

It is to this image that thousands of believers continually flock in order to give offerings and make requests for everything under the sun; the girl next door, cures for diseases, physical beauty, male children, examination passes, better jobs, first prize in the national lottery.

Many are the stories of requests granted. These draw in more and more believers.

The image can be investigated.

The monk associated with this image has the appearance of a man in his late forties with a beaming Siamese face and a dark robe. He says his name is Sorn. This means, "arrow".

Just over two hundred and forty years ago, during the confusion and chaos of the destruction of Ayudhya by the Burmese, he decided to leave his body. He can be seen sitting cross-legged in front of the dark bronze image he has chosen. As he dies, a very bright ball of light exits his body at the front, just above the navel. It enters the image. At the time of his death he says he was a non-returner.

Now his Centre is very large, brilliant white, and fills most of his torso. He can leave the image at will and make his form any size he wishes. He says he is now an Arahant and appears here from Nibbāna to "promote Buddhism and help beings cure mental and physical suffering by increasing their faith." *

> How long will he stay?
> *He smiles.*
> How long will Chachoengsao be safe?
> *As long as he is there.*
> So, how long will he stay?
> *He looks into the distance and says nothing.*
> And the winning lottery ticket?
> He smiles.
> *If their previous karma is good enough, they win it. If not, they don't.*

By using the latent potential of the Centre and the tools that come out of it, we verify these things for ourselves and make up our own minds about them. Therefore, we need not rely on having to choose among all the various points of view that clamour for our attention and acceptance.

If we cannot verify these things for ourselves, we suspend judgement and get on with our practice.

---

* Compare Jesus: *Thy Faith hath made thee whole.*

30. MORE BODIES

We have a physical body about which we have learned enough to manage pretty well. But we don't know much about it. When we try to learn more, we get involved in an ever-expanding medical and scientific jargon, which presents a new language of its own. There is a mass of detail and detailed labelling which tells us more and more about smaller and smaller.

It's like going further and further into the nuts and bolts and electrical wires and fuses and fuel pipes and callipers and tyre treads and emission system of a motor car and neglecting to give more than a cursory glance at the chap holding the steering wheel.

Current medical philosophy and language depend upon an interpretation of the body's workings that is almost entirely materialistic.

It therefore devolves increasingly into chemistry, surgery, and transplants. In all of this there is money to be made. Giant international companies take advantage by selling products, many of which have been tested not on humans but on animals. These, despite the efforts of heavy advertising, usually do not produce any particular benefits and often have undesirable side effects. Especially for the animals. But for us too.

What we cannot learn from current medical philosophy is that there is more to this body than just a physical machine that exhibits livingness.

"Livingness"- Life - is something which current medical

science (and philosophy) cannot explain even though it is the most noticeable characteristic of a living being. Which is why we get so excited if that particular characteristic disappears.

If current medical philosophy, and the current scientific opinions upon which it is based, is compelled to offer an explanation, it suggests some kind of "happy accident" which happened some time ago in an evolving material universe and which requires more research, which will need more funds, which will come, ultimately, out of our pockets.

However much of our money they play with, they will never find the "secret" of life because they look further and further and deeper and deeper in the wrong direction. You cannot find out what colour hat you are wearing by looking up your arse. You cannot even see if you are wearing a hat at all.

The physical human body functions as a living being only as long as it is inhabited by, and impregnated with, an astral body which can provide a non-physical link between it and the origin of life which is the Centre.

It can function as a machine during temporary astral absence unless a major physical component (heart, brain etc.) breaks down. In this case the astral will return to find "its" body dead and perhaps already cremated.

This is a source of sorrow (astrals can feel sorrow) and bewilderment and is one reason why astrals hang around a place appearing, to those who can see them, as ghosts.

The astral provides livingness by means of the sushumnā and subsidiary centres which themselves derive from another body inside the astral body. This is the "deva" body. This derives from yet another body inside it, the brahmā body.

Inside the brahmā body there are two possibilities.

One is that there are no more forms; just subtle and all-pervading formless worlds – planes of being – which encircle the plane of Nibbāna. Out of Nibbāna they came and into it again they will return.

The other possibility is a fifth body, a seated Buddha with a transparent white centre. Entering this centre, one's separateness disappears into the vast no-thingness of page 15.

This makes five bodies that have forms: one material and four mental.

It helps if one thinks of these five bodies fitting inside one another like a set of Russian dolls. Each is the result of karmic actions, in some cases a very long time ago.

When one learned how to create a lighted sphere at the Centre and succeeded in entering it (see chapter 16), one acquired a method whereby one can enter sphere after sphere in succession, getting closer and closer to the original state of non-becoming in which all rebirth and every conceivable form of suffering and unsatisfactoriness ceases.

In the early stages of this process one can (but need not) have a form that corresponds to the inhabitants of the level of reality (world) one has entered. In the final stage, one has no form. One experiences Nibbāna, the changeless state, the highest form of happiness.

Similarly, one can use the lighted sphere at the Centre to

enable one to investigate the astral body in one's physical body. Illuminating the inside of the physical body, one can see the astral body inside.

The form of the astral body is commonly a younger version of the physical body at that time. But it could also be the form of one's previous life (especially while one is still a baby and hasn't, as it were, "settled" into the new life). It could be the form of a deva (angel) if one had been reborn from a heaven world, or an astral or even an animal if one had been any of these last time round.

Looking carefully, one can see the subsidiary centres and the sushumnā inside it although it is not possible at this stage to be sure whether these form part of the astral body or not. To do this one has to exit the physical body in the astral and look back at the physical.

One can "enter" the astral body consciously. That is to say, one is able to withdraw into it from the physical body.

When one withdraws into it, one gives up (temporarily) the gross material body that it energises, the physical world it inhabits and the five senses which come with it. One thereby acquires the astral eye and the ability to see the astral bodies of others when they are in their physical bodies. One can also see them when they are not – i.e. when they are astral travelling or they are physically dead.

One discovers that one's astral body has astral senses including the "Third Eye" which can be used to contact the astral plane of being. The astral body can also act independently of the physical body.

That is to say, when one has withdrawn into the astral body, one can exit the physical body. One can do this through the aperture of brahma, the occipital aperture or, simply, by just deciding to move forward and out of the body. Then one will find oneself standing or sitting near one's physical body and able to see it quite clearly as something separate from what one is experiencing as one's self at that moment.

At this point, one can see that, when exiting the physical body as an astral, one takes with one the Centre, the subsidiary centres and the nadis, leaving the physical body "empty" until one returns. Kundalini, however, in its latent (sleeping) state, remains with the physical body in the perineum.

Having exited like this, one can astral travel. (See chapter 28).

Just as one discovered, while in the physical body, how to see the astral body inside one, so in the astral body one can, when one looks, see that there is another body inside the astral body.

One can do this while in the astral body but without exiting the physical body. This has the advantage that one does not have to concern oneself with maintaining a link with the physical body. On the other hand, exiting the bodies makes their "emptiness" very obvious.

This body commonly has the form of a deva, a sage, a yogi, or an inhabitant of the lower heaven worlds. It includes those whose practice is spiritual progress and who are endeavouring to move up ever higher, for example Stream-enterers and Once-returners. These worlds can be investigated in this body.

This body can be called the "deva body".

Just as one withdrew from the physical body into the

astral body, so, now, one can withdraw from the astral body into the deva body. Having done so, one looks back and sees that, from the point of view where one is now, the astral body is empty. But it does contain the subsidiary centres. These have been left behind.

The Centre, however, remains with the deva body. Its colour is usually a bright white because of the increased purity of this body.

The deva body can see astrals, although normally they cannot see a deva unless he wills that they should.

It can be used to explore the level of reality on which it exists and to communicate with other beings that exist on that level. This can be illuminating since one can find out what kind of activity these beings practised to achieve rebirth on this level. Unlike oneself who is at this time a kind of "tourist", since one still has a physical (and astral) body to return to.

Once again if, while in the deva body, one looks inside, one can see another body. This is the brahmā body which, dependent on the tradition in which one conceptualises one's ideas on these things, is likely to appear as a kind of demigod. Entering this, one gains access to the brahmā realm of existence and its inhabitants. (See chapter 29).

With the exception of the gross physical body, these are mental bodies. Therefore, their appearance can be changed to something else by mental intention. Though, in the absence of such an intention, they have, as it were, a default setting (appearance) dependent on an individual's previous karma.

Each of them contains the same Centre, though its colour may differ from body to body. As the bodies become more refined, the Centre will appear progressively brighter.

One understands clearly how it is that all beings originate from the same Centre. Their forms, as it were, are strung on strings (tentacles), see page 22, which go right back into the origin of everything.

One sees that the road home leads ever further and further inward into oneself rather than outward into the increasingly material forms of outer bodies.

In withdrawing inward to more refined forms, one is in fact retracing one's steps. This is the way all beings have come on their journey outwards from the Centre via subtle mental forms into the labyrinth of material evolution. The spider, the amoeba, the archangel and you are all fellow travellers on this journey from a single departure point. Who could have predicted it?

Even though the physical body remains alive while one explores the worlds of the other bodies, it is not always easy to remain in contact with it.

One developed the physical eye in order to see physical forms, so it is difficult for the astral eye to see the material world clearly. The deva eye can see the astral world clearly but finds it hard to see the material world, which seems faint and vague. Normally, the brahmā form does not see or have any awareness of our material world. Consequently, he has no interest in it.

However, if a brahmā wishes to contact our world, he can take on a deva form which, being mental, can have any appearance he wishes. Under certain conditions, he can also enter a living physical being, much as an astral can sometimes enter someone else's physical body even if someone else's "own" astral body is "in residence".

The physical body is constantly changing, though relatively slowly. One can *make* it change in directions that one desires by dieting, exercising etc.

With the mental bodies, however, although they have "default settings", one can choose to take on any form one likes. Instantaneously. Time is not a factor. One can also surround oneself with a mentally created world. Initially this will be an environment that is related to one's previous karma. But as soon as one realises that it is a purely mental creation, one has the potential ability to create whatever world on that level one wishes.

This is similar to the experience many have when they *realise* that they are dreaming, actually during the dream. So long as they can hold on to that realisation, they can dream whatever they want to. Many find this an exhilarating and liberating experience (one can jump off the tops of buildings).

It is similar to genuine astral travel (one can pass through walls) and is often confused with it. But the conscious awareness in dreams is generally so dim that even the most fantastic and unlikely events can occur without one realising how extraordinary they are until one wakes up.

With some individuals, a fifth body is found inside the brahmā form. This is a seated Buddha with a large Centre which is white, clear and empty. Entering this, one has temporarily gone beyond all noumenal and phenomenal existence to a state upstream of all conditions or duality (see page 16, and then page 15).

31. KUNDALINI

"Kundalini" comes from Sanskrit and means "coiled" or "the coiled one". Visually (to the inner eye), it appears as a snake with its head resting on three (sometimes seven) coils. It has yellow scales tinged with red and yellow at the edges and red eyes. Its centre is a deep reddish brown, radiating sensual desire (i.e. strong desire for sense contacts). Inside this centre is the brahmā form from which it originates. Inside the brahmā is an empty (clear, colourless) centre.

Kundalini is found in the Base Chakra. The Centre can both activate the Base Chakra and wake up Kundalini. Kundalini, when awoken, can be drawn up through the sushumnā with the inbreaths.

When the serpent enters the sushumnā, its form dissolves into a highly charged flow of energy. As it ascends, this activates, in order, each of the subsidiary centres until it reaches the Crown Chakra. On its way, it cannot activate the Centre, which is not located in the sushumnā.

The energy can be made to flow up continuously. When it reaches the Crown Chakra, it fills it and the feeling is heavy and thick. If the energy is allowed to flow out from the Crown Chakra and out of the body, the heavy feeling in the Crown Chakra disappears. The flow of energy, from the Base Chakra to the Crown Chakra and out of the body, can continue indefinitely.

This flow of energy can also be allowed to rain down within the body from the inside of the top of the head like a fountain, energising the whole body via the nadis.

COMMUNICATING WITH KUNDALINI

If one activates the Third-Eye Chakra, one can cause Kundalini to appear to the inner eye and one can communicate with him.

One tends to associate communication with sound waves or written symbols. But this is *secondary* communication. In all the levels of being above those that require material bodies, one communicates by mentally creating a thought or intention.

Communications which one *receives* on these higher levels are either perceived directly as mental concepts or are "heard", even though there are no sound waves (consider music heard in a dream or even while day-dreaming).

> Who are you?
> *Lord of Creation.*
> What were you before?
> *Brahmā.*

> Why did you become Kundalini?
> *Desire to create.*
> What is your desire now?
> *To be united with Siva* (the Crown Chakra).

Still using the Third-Eye Chakra, one can start with the image of Kundalini as he appears now and go back on his time-track to his origin. This process is very similar to winding back a reel of film in order to locate an earlier episode in the story. So long as the film is intact and one has a suitable viewer (in this case the mind), one can reel back all the way to the beginning.

At the beginning of Kundalini's story, a snake's head bursts out of the earth followed by its whole body.

If one goes back before his birth in matter, one discovers a formless brahmā, who made an "adhitthāna", "a resolution to create".

> Why? *Desire.*
> Does Kundalini know about Indra? *Yes.*
> Does he know about the Buddha? *Yes.*
> Does he know about the Buddha's teachings? *Yes.*
> So? *Not interested.*
> Is he content with things as they are? *Yes.*

Where does Kundalini get his energy from? From matter. As Kundalini, he is permanently linked to matter like a pipe to a reservoir. His present form, therefore, will endure as long as the material universe but will not survive the destruction of matter at the end of a kalpa (world cycle). Why take on the form of a snake? Easy and convenient. Nothing sticks out to form an impediment as it insinuates its way along.

He has become the embodiment of desire in matter which feeds upon itself like an *ouroboros*, the snake that eternally bites and tries to eat its own tail. Because of the closed system which this creates, his desire is eternally insatiable. Hence his longing for union with Siva in the Crown Chakra is an attempt to escape from the duality in which he finds himself (see pages 22/23) and re-establish unity.

How does he *know* there is anything higher to be desired? Because his origins are in the brahmā world from which his desire caused him to fall away. He is indeed a Fallen Angel.

One can see the significance here of why it is that, when the astral body exits the physical body, it takes with it all the subsidiary centres, including the Base Chakra. *But not Kundalini.* The astral body with its centres derive from the Centre itself, i.e. from a plane of being which is upstream of matter. Hence astrals do not experience material sensual desires.

One can verify this by experiment. One can enter the astral body but remain within the physical body. By activating the Desire Chakra, one can induce a strong sensual desire. Then one exits the physical body.

Immediately the strong sensual feeling disappears. If one looks back at the physical body one has just vacated, one can see quite clearly that Kundalini is still there in the perineum. Re-entering the physical body restores the physical feeling of sensuality.

All this explains why it is that many yogis, who use Kundalini and promote its "union" with the Crown Chakra, make no mention of the Centre. Since Kundalini cannot activate it, they cannot see it. The consequence is that, because they attribute so much importance to a *material* energy, their concepts of reality are fundamentally tinged with sensuality. They cannot therefore conceive of Liberation, which involves going utterly beyond and upstream of the material senses.

What happens to them is that they start off *using* Kundalini to awaken the centres and acquire higher levels of consciousness up to the Crown Chakra, but end up being overpowered by Kundalini and being drawn down into the realm of sensual pleasure of which he is master. In Buddhist terms, they end up in Māra's net.

The Centre, the ultimate release from desire and suffering,

is upstream of everything else in the universe, including Kundalini. Kundalini is just one manifestation of the Centre's infinite latent tendencies that appeared in matter via the brahmā world.

The Centre is linked to all the subsidiary centres which derive from it and provides them with energy and livingness. These subsidiary centres (but not the Centre) are also linked to each other via the sushumnā.

They energise the major organs within their immediate vicinity.

Branching out from them are the nadis and Kundalini can energise these via the subsidiary centres.

AWAKENING AND RAISING KUNDALINI

Kundalini is innate in matter, waiting to be awakened. Although it originates from the Centre, when it is used to activate the other centres via the sushumnā, it has no effect on the Centre itself.

Moving the sphere (gold or white) from the Centre down to the Base Chakra, one activates that centre. This is the element of Earth. It appears yellow. Within it is seen Kundalini, sleeping. One awakens Kundalini using the light of the sphere and feels the powerful turbulating energy spreading out through the nadis to infuse the lower body.

On the inbreath, one draws Kundalini out of the Base Chakra into the sushumnā and up to the Desire Chakra. This centre is a milky off-white which becomes red when activated. This is the element of Water. Kundalini activates this centre and strong waves of sensual desire are felt which affect the sexual organs. Images may appear which correspond to these feelings.

Kundalini is drawn further up the sushumnā into the Solar Plexus Chakra, which it activates. This centre is red. This is the element of Fire. Waves of heat spread out from this centre, which is the source of the vital heat, throughout the body.

Kundalini is drawn further up to the Heart Chakra from which, when it is activated, strong feelings of a soothing, tender love and affection are felt in the chest area and beyond. This centre is blue. This is the element of Air.

When Kundalini is drawn up to the Throat Chakra and activates it, it is seen to be purple. This is the element of Ether. One perceives a sense of purification in one's body and a feeling of being able to interact and communicate with others. This replaces the feeling of rivalry (see page 21). In fact, if you purify rivalry, you always find it transmutes into co-operation.

The next stage is the activating of the Brain Chakra. This is yellow. There is an intense awareness of the clarity of thought and a feeling that one can understand anything to which one turns one's mind.

When Kundalini enters the Third-Eye Centre, it is seen to be dazzling white or shining blue. This produces *vision*, a higher manifestation of understanding. The divine eye is opened and one can see beings from other worlds and levels of being. One has a sense of power and realises that whatever one wants to see will appear if one makes a resolution to see it. One can see the former lives of oneself and others.

Drawing Kundalini up to activate the occipital or Spirit

Chakra reveals it as dark blue.

Activating it fills one's whole body with positive feelings. One experiences the four brahmavihāras.*

It is possible for consciousness to exit the body via this center through the aperture where the two parietal bones meet (and join) the occipital bone.

Finally, Kundalini is drawn up to reach the Crown Chakra, which has always been its goal. The colour of this centre is grey and golden. It is filled with concentrated bliss and deep peace. It feels like the final destination of a long journey that seems to have been going on forever. It seems that nothing other than this could possibly be desired.

It is obvious why those who have reached this point after such a long journey should think it is the ultimate, the highest, the supreme. In fact, it is not. It still has the characteristic of impermanence.

There can be found many Buddha images in which the Buddha is seen sitting on (typically) three coils of a snake (a cobra). Above his head appears its hood which overspreads his head, as though protecting him.

This represents Kundalini after it has been awakened fully and completed its journey up the sushumnā to the seat of Siva, the Crown Chakra.

Some have interpreted this as showing that the raising of Kundalini can bring about enlightenment such as that of the Buddha.

---

* *Four brahmavihāras: The four resting places of Brahmā; loving kindness, compassion, sympathetic joy, equanimity.*

In the early suttas, which contain the most accurate record of the Buddha's own words, there is nothing to justify this belief. It entered Buddhism from Hinduism and Brahmanism at a later date when the Mahayana Sect was developing.

This experience may be prolonged but it has a beginning and an ending. However long Kundalini remains here, he will, in the end, fall away from this state back into matter.

If one wishes, one can continuously raise Kundalini up from the Base Chakra through the sushumnā to the Crown Chakra where it will gradually spread out at the top of the head and flow back down through the body like a fountain, percolating through the cells of the body to the Base Chakra, there to rise again.

It can be made to circulate in this way, rising on the inbreath and subsiding on the outbreath for as long as one wishes (though not for ever). All the while, there is a sense of exaltation and poise as the physical body is filled with bliss. One experiences the satisfaction of coming back home.

There are variations on this. One can visualise not only the centres but also the myriad of nadis which spread out from them in all directions and permeate the whole physical body. Drawing the Kundalini energy out to flow back through these as well can have an invigorating and healing effect on the physical cells through which they pass.

It would seem that this might be a way to levitate the physical body. I have not verified this.

It is also possible to draw the energy, but not Kundalini himself, *out of* the body into space through the aperture of brahma. When this is done, the sushumnā pipe feels cleansed and open at both ends to the Void. Body and mind feel purified and, although the physical body is clearly perceived, there is no sense at all of material heaviness or the inertia of matter.

It is also possible to use the Centre to activate the centres instead of Kundalini. The process is much the same except that the sushumnā is not used. The fine, non-physical light thread (brahmā channel) which joins all the centres to the Centre is used instead. Effectively, one is working within the astral body and consequently none of the strong physical feelings and sensations experienced when using Kundalini are felt.

This method also makes it possible to activate the centre *outside* of the body and a few inches above the head, the Brahmā Chakra.

IT IS POSSIBLE TO ENTER KUNDALINI

Make the centres visible to the inner eye. Locate the Base Chakra. It is a pale greenish yellow. Enter the sphere. Kundalini is there, with you, in the sphere. Yellow and red and green with red eyes.

Enter Kundalini. You have the form of the snake. You have *become* Kundalini. You feel full of a restless, moving, *wanting* energy: ready to act. Push out into the sushumnā. The snake form, your form, dissolves as you enter it into a continuous flow of powerful energy.

Enter the Desire Chakra. You feel turbulating energy which awakens the Desire Chakra and stimulates corresponding images.

Move up the sushumnā. Enter the Solar Plexus Chakra.

The feeling is of solid energy. You can see the vast network of nadis.

Move on up and enter the Heart Chakra. The feeling is that of a full water container ready to overflow with the water of the heart, cool and fresh. There is an image of two birds perched next to each other.

Up to the Throat Chakra. Enter it. A feeling of peace and a vision of an empty battlefield.

To the Brain Chakra, where the feeling is of inexpressible clarity of mind and the image of oneself sitting peacefully on a verandah.

To the Spirit Chakra; a sense of complete freedom experienced and an image of monks with serene faces.

To the Third-Eye Chakra; a feeling of peace and a view of lighted spheres moving endlessly out and away before disappearing into space.

To the Crown Chakra: peace, happiness, bliss. An image of a mountain peak covered in snow. This is Mount Meru.

Leaving the body through the aperture of brahma, one leaves Kundalini behind. One moves into a spinning, clear, deep blue, soothing sphere. It feels ready to be used and one feels ready to use it; to emanate peace and healing throughout the universe.

Note: During the ascent, strong physical feelings may be felt in the two lowest centres. In the Solar Plexus Chakra, the feeling is half physical, half non-physical. From the heart centre upward, there are no feelings or awareness which relate directly to a physical body.

32. LONGEVITY

In the Generation of Adam, we read:

> "And Adam begat Seth
> and Seth begat Enos
> and Enos begat Cainan
> and Cainan begat Mahalaleel
> and Cainan lived eight hundred and forty years
> after he begat Mahalaleel..."

Furthermore:

> ... all the days of Methuselah were nine hundred sixty and nine years: and he died.

We may make what we like of this assertion about the length of Cainan's life and Methuselah's life.

But it is clear that, with the Rejuvenation Cycle (see page 79*ff*), one has gone beyond healing to actual renewal of the body's cells. This is very likely to extend one's life. This is going to depend upon firstly, the state of the body when one begins Rejuvenation and, secondly, one's ability to generate and deploy the healing and warming light at will. Upon one's mental powers in fact. Mind comes first.

There is an enormous difference between individuals as to what they can and cannot do. But their individual abilities do not affect whether something is *possible* or not. The Channel was always swimmable. It's just that nobody did it until Captain Webb came along.

In 1909, Webb's elder brother Thomas unveiled a memorial to him. On it the short inscription reads:

"Nothing great is easy."

33. THE PHILOSOPHER'S STONE

Until the beginnings of modern chemistry, alchemy, which preceded it, was primarily concerned with the search for the philosopher's stone. This was believed to make it possible to transmute base metals into gold and to confer immortality. Despite claims that this has been achieved, none of them meets modern standards for verification.

In the Maha-Parinibbāna Sutta, the Buddha explains to Ānanda that a Buddha can, if he chooses, continue his worldly existence (i.e. with a flesh and blood body) until the end of the kalpa.

"And the Blessed One said: Whosoever, Ānanda, has developed, practised, employed, strengthened, maintained, scrutinized, and brought to perfection the four constituents of psychic power* can, if he so desires, remain throughout a world-period or until the end of it.

"The Tathāgata**, Ānanda, has done so. Therefore, the Tathāgata could, if he so desired, remain throughout a kalpa or until the end of it."

How long is a kalpa?

"Imagine a huge empty cube at the beginning of a kalpa, approximately 16 miles square on each side. Once every

---

* Iddhipāda
** Tathāgata: *the name the Buddha used when referring to himself. Literally, the "Thus Gone".*

100 years, you insert a tiny mustard seed into the cube. The huge cube will be filled even before the kalpa ends."

Buddha does not mean by living "to the end of a kalpa", physical immortality. A kalpa comes to an end with the end of the physical universe. He means that he can continue to live a physical existence so long as there is a supply of matter to support the ongoing regeneration of his body. When that supply runs out, his body cannot survive.

In the event he chose not to. What makes life worth living is not its number of years but its quality.

> "Now I am frail, Ānanda, old, aged, far gone in years. This is my eightieth year, and my life is spent. Even as an old cart, Ānanda, is held together with much difficulty, so the body of the Tathāgata is kept going only with supports. It is, Ānanda, only when the Tathāgata, disregarding external objects, with the cessation of certain feelings, attains to and abides in the signless concentration of mind, that his body is more comfortable."

Consequently,
> "At the Capala shrine, the Tathāgata renounced his will to live on, with inward calm and joy."

Thus the Buddha sets the ultimate limit obtainable by rejuvenation and also the undesirability of attaining those limits, since:

> "All compounded things are transient.
> They are subject to arising and passing away.
> Having come into existence they vanish;
> Good is the Peace when they cease forever."

Nibbāna is the Highest Happiness.

*"There is a Blind Buddha in your belly.
Wake him up!"*

34. CREATIVITY AND THE CENTRE

The Centre is the source of all creation. Creativity comes from the Centre. It may however, manifest in a subsidiary centre, using the original impulse and energy which always originates in the Centre. This is *centrifugal*.

All activity, unimpeded, is drawn towards the Centre. It may however appear to aim for a subsidiary centre and stop short there. It will never find lasting satisfaction doing this. This is *centripetal*.

Therefore, one's own creativity and the creativity of others are alternative ways of homing in on the Centre.

They can also, more easily, enable one to home in on subsidiary centres in the first instance.

If one is creative oneself, one creates from experience of a particular centre.

If one responds to the creativity of others, this can lead one to experience the centre from which that creator worked.

Reading **poetry** stimulates the centres. Poets like Keats stimulate the Heart Chakra. Pope stimulates the Throat and Brain Chakras. Byron stimulates Heart, Throat and Brain. Shelley, particularly in *Adonais,* stimulates the Centre.

Poetry which stimulates a particular centre was written when the poet was conscious of that centre. Or because stimulation from a sense object had temporarily awakened that centre.

Painting like that of Goya stimulates the Desire Chakra. That of Constable and Turner the Heart. Pre-Raphaelites the Desire and Base Chakras. I do not know of any painters who have successfully communicated the Centre although I do know of painters who have tried. Only a few of Blake's paintings and some modern abstract paintings seem likely to stimulate the Centre.

In former times, religious art which seems likeliest to stimulate the Centre, was rarely signed and the artists are therefore unknown. This fitted in with a concept that art was inspiration from God or the Muses and it was not the artist's role to interpose himself between the inspired work and its observers. His task was, like that of a prophet or healer, to offer himself as a vehicle.

In modern times, the concept of the artist and his work as in some way separate is a fundamental dualism and obstacle.

In both ancient and modern times, painting rarely throws off the limitations of its dependence upon images and material objects. Even when it is using them as visual mirrors of intellectual concepts.

This becomes clearer by comparison with a parallel to this in the development of **mathematics**.

There are those who have learned to count using stones. They calculate: 'One stone plus two stones equals three stones.' Having acquired some skill in this, they move on to more complicated calculations. For which they need more stones. The better they are at this, the bigger the sack of stones they have to carry around with them.

In order to push mathematical science further, they need to detach number from object. Firstly, the objects used (the stones) are replaced by *symbols*. These are figures which can be inscribed. Because they are symbols they acquire an abstract identity distinct from their role in referring to apples or marbles (or stones). We can dispense with the stones (and the sack) and get along with sheets of paper. These are more manageable but we are able to dispense even with these.

The medium is refined still further and we arrive at the computer.

There are two kinds of computer: the brain and an inferior external imitation of this that can be held in the hand. Neither of these is 100% reliable. But it is a big step forward.

However, to move on to a level of mathematics which enables you to contact and experience the Centre and the mind to understand it, it is necessary to detach number from its fundamental duality. You cannot count things, even in your mind, if there are no things or concepts to count.

To detach abstract number from refined mental integers (numbers), you have to upstream (see chapter 22) to a higher plane and calculate that:

A. **1 + 1 = 1**

There is only one calculation more fundamental than this:

B. **1 + 1 = 1 = 0**

(where **0** is not nothing but the source and sum of all possible integers including itself.)

(See chapters 1, 2 & 3.)

In order to illustrate the endless cycle of rebirth in the Sangsara, this can be extended thus:

The way in which the beings, worlds, universes come and go within this structure can be expressed:

C. $0 = (+1 -1) = 0$

(where **+1** is the beginning/birth of anything and **−1** is its end/death. The brackets ( ) represent everything that occurs to that "anything" between its beginning and its end.)

When the "anythings" are seen as every thing it appears thus:

D. $0 = (+1 -1) = 0 = (+1 -1) = 0 = (+1 -1) = 0 = (+1 -1) = 0$ *ad infinitum.*

No individual entity (self) of any kind passes over or through from bracket to bracket. The motivating energy force ("following wind") is Desire. The detail is provided by Karma and latent karma. When it is realised that each and every bracket contains the whole of each and every lifetime. It shows clearly that everything gained and experienced = everything lost. Nothing is saved. All that continues is the mistaken desire for more births (and deaths). The horror of eternal existence in the world(s) of form (the Sangsāra) is clearly visible. And also the wonderful underlying Truth that **0** = Eternal Peace.

Sculpture has been almost more successful. In ancient times, a successful stone representation of this profound equation (A) appeared in a form which is usually called a *linga* (a Sanskrit word meaning "mark" or "sign" that also appears as *lingam*). In many very old Indian temples, there was, and sometimes still is, an inner sanctum in which you would have found a single linga and nothing else. After the completion of his education, a suitable initiate was led to the door of this sanctum by his hierophant and ushered inside alone, and in silence, and left there until he chose to come out or died.

He had been led to believe that he would experience the Divine Presence. If his understanding was sufficiently mature, his mind, in response to the presence of this powerful symbol, would make the transition from duality to at-one-ment and complete his enlightenment.

Since ancient times, degeneration has occurred here. Priests have taken over, whose experience and understanding have reached no further than awakening Kundalini in the Base Chakra in a way which involves the Desire Chakra (see pages 163/164) and leading it up to reach the Brain and Crown Chakras. They have interpreted these representations of non-duality as stylised phalluses and have led their neophytes into thinking (and practices) involving the Desire Chakra to a degree that is not conducive to rediscovery of the non-dualistic and non-material Centre.

Music is essentially dualistic. You need at least two notes to make a melody. The ordinary impatient person will not normally be content with such a basic point/counterpoint melody.

There have been attempts to refine this to a single note alternating with silence. For most lovers of music this produces an effect similar to Chinese water torture in which drops of water fall at fixed intervals on the forehead of the victim until he is willing to tell his torturers anything they want to know. Even making the intervals irregular does not take us much further.

There have also been attempts to make music from a single continuous note. Some of the centres emit a continuous note. But a continuous note is still itself dualistic, being a wave-like vibration. In any case, a single note, to communicate a meaning, needs an ear. Back again to duality.

There have been occasional performances in which an orchestra, having taken their places, sit still and unmoving.

Despite John Cage's efforts with "Four thirty-three" in 1952, these have never been entirely successful. Only at a first performance will the audience be completely unsuspecting. With such an audience, the silence does indeed grow. Some members of it may experience a mild satori. Most will feel a growing and potentially explosive frustration (they have paid good money for the seats they sit in). Eventually, the 'deception' is perceived and the concert hall gradually erupts into an unrehearsed discordant cacophony that is entirely pluralistic.

After this, if the management wishes to avoid physical damage to the concert hall, it will have arranged something more conventional. Preferably Mozart. There is nothing better than Mozart or Bach to soothe unsettled and aggravated brains and minds. Which is presumably why, in accordance with the perversity of human nature, they are not played continuously in lunatic asylums.

It would be very effective.

35. OTHER METHODS

The aim is twofold: to become aware of the Centre and to realise the significance of what it is.

You are climbing a mountain. You miss your footing and fall. In the space between the slipping foot and the jerk when your rope snaps taut and leaves you hanging there alive, you may perceive a surge of energy from the area around the Centre.

You are between nine and ten years old. You are smoking your first Woodbine with your friends in a disused air-raid shelter. You experience something like a crackle of lightning in your brain and awareness drops to the Centre. You all giggle helplessly.

You turn your car over and climb uninjured from the wreckage and look around. A great wave of well-being spreads out from the Centre. You don't know whether to laugh or cry. You laugh (see page 72).

There are many other incidents of similar awakening. They are always evanescent. The flow of life resumes. Awareness is drawn back into it. Even the memory all but disappears because of its irrelevance to everyday living, which is assumed to be (but isn't) the *important* business of life.

36. REMEMBERING PAST LIVES

There are those who say they would like to believe in past lives but cannot. What they mean is that they don't *want* to remember and therefore they *will* not believe. Being ignorant of the truth, they persuade themselves into believing what they wish to believe.

The reason is that the past has good times and bad times. Sometimes one does not want to remember the good times if they were very good because it is unbearable that they are gone forever. Sometimes one does not want to remember the bad times because one cannot confront the mental and physical pain. Often one does not want to remember those things one has done to the disadvantage of others. (Think of Stalin, Attila, slaughterhouse men.) This is a matter of attempting to stifle the conscience.

Each and every life started with a birth that was painful and ended with a death that was usually painful and unwanted.

Most people find a barrier when they remember back; the birth. In addition, they become aware that, if there was a past life, before that birth was a death. There were also nine months in the womb, which was progressively uncomfortable and cramped. They may not want to remember these things.

Nevertheless, if one is ever to come to recall or re-experience these things so that understanding can dawn and one can take charge of one's destiny, one will have to confront them.

The biggest barrier is conscience. Until one admits that one is wrong, one cannot begin to think of how to put things right.

If you have mastered use of the lighted sphere, remembering past lives is not difficult.

The most straightforward method is to use the Centre to activate the Third-Eye Chakra (see chapter 24). One can use it as one uses the physical eyes or one can actually enter it.

If one enters it, one makes an intention to locate an incident when one was a child. When an incident has been located, one *moves* to the incident and examines enough of the detail to get good recall.

Then one intends (makes an intention) to locate an incident when one was a small baby. When one has located such an incident, one *moves* to the incident and examines the detail.

Next, one locates an incident when one was in one's mother's womb.

One then moves to it. The first time one does this, the effect is very powerful. The water, the discomfort, the curious noises are so obviously genuine.

Next one locates an incident just *before* one entered one's mother's womb. When this has been found, one moves to it. Since, often, one is an astral just before entering the womb, that is what one will find.

One will have an astral form that corresponds to the physical form of one's previous birth. Though it will not necessarily be identical to how one looked at death. It will normally be how the *astral* looked when one was on one's deathbed – a younger version of the dying physical. At this stage, one can sometimes remember one's name.

Next, one locates the incident when one had just died. One moves to that. Often, one will be near the dead body looking at it. One may be aware of others nearby. If one tries to communicate with them, one fails because they are probably unable to see astrals.

Next, one locates an incident just before one dies and moves to that. One will find oneself dying or, if the death was, for example, the result of an accident, one will find oneself in the sequence of events which led up to the accident. Driving in a car, perhaps. Or stepping off the pavement. From here, one can move *forward* to the actual point of death, if one wants to, and experience that. But one doesn't need to and it may restimulate in the present physical body any pain which one might have suffered.

From here, one can go back further into the previous birth to incidents such as "the day you got married" or "when you were at school". In each case, you *move* back to the incident so that you can experience it just as it was, though not of course with the same *intensity* as the original incidents. After all, you are really experiencing a facsimile of what occurred. It is like watching a film that was taken of something that actually happened.

You can't watch the actual event because that belongs to the past and doesn't exist any more. But you *can* watch the film as many times as you like. Each time through, you will notice more and more detail in terms of, for example, what people were wearing, furniture, locations. You can identify relatives, friends (or enemies).

Remembering back in this way, in a series of jumps, rather

than examining every detail – every painful birth, every unwanted death – you can avoid areas which you are not comfortable about confronting yet. You can always go back to them later if and when you want to and have developed a certain detachment.

Once you can do this, the key to your past and your origins is in your hands. You can continue going back as far as you like. You will not always have been a human. You have been animal, insect, bird, deva (angel). The list is endless. You can jump in bigger leaps – go back two lives at once, twenty lives. It is up to you.

You can make an intention to remember an incident when you were a monk. Or a soldier. Or a king. Or a cat. Mostly, there will be one. You *move* back to it and you can move from it, forward or backward to acquire more detail of that life. For example, locate an incident when the monk was meditating, or the king was crowned, or the soldier was fighting, or the cat had kittens.

This sequence of birth and death of which you have been a part, and still are, and of which you will continue to be a part until you manage to escape, is called the Sangsāra, literally the "perpetual wandering". In this unbroken sequence of cause and effect, we arise now here and now there in accordance with our deeds and their effects, our karma.

The Buddha has said:

> "From an inconceivable beginning comes this Sangsāra. A beginning point is not seen. Beings, hindered by ignorance and fettered by craving, wander on. Long have you thus experienced stress, experienced pain, experienced loss, filling the cemeteries — long enough to become disenchanted

with all fabricated things, long enough to become dispassionate, long enough to seek release."

He also told Vacchagotta that he could recollect ninety-one kalpas. How long is a kalpa? (See page 174). But that was still not the beginning.

There is no beginning point, just as there is no beginning point in a circle.

You have never before tried this tracking back. It may take time to get the hang of it. Certainly, you need good, sustained concentration. All the information is accessible. It is stored in mind. Most of it is not stored in brain, though there are tools in the brain that can help to organise it.

It is certainly a lot easier if you do this with someone else who can act as a prompter:

> "Locate an incident when you were.......
> When was it?
> Move to the incident and tell me when you are there.
> What can you see?"
> Et cetera.

This helps your concentration and prevents your mind wandering off.

If you can do this, it is also possible to access the previous lives of others. The method is the same as that used to discover the origins of Kundalini. (See page 162*ff*).

It is similar to going to a deserted beach and finding a single line of footprints. If you follow the prints back in the direction they are coming from, you will find the place where the maker of the prints first stepped onto the sand.

Similarly, if you can mentally grasp the image of someone, which shows his "footprint" or self at a particular point in time, you can go back on his time track as far as it exists. Locate an incident when he was a young man. Move to the incident. Locate an incident when he was a baby. Move to the incident. Locate an incident before he entered his mother's womb. Move to that incident. Et cetera.

Doing this helps us to understand why children can be very different from their parents or their brothers and sisters, even though their upbringing and education might have been the same.

It is fashionable to believe that a newborn baby is a brand new being, who may have genetic conditioning, but is otherwise a blank canvas.

Politically, this is useful because the voters can be encouraged to believe that if poor children had the same opportunities (schools, education, encouragement) as rich children, they would do just as well. If not better.

However, not all the children of middle-class, European teachers reached the same heights as the young Mozart, who played at an exhibition before royalty at five and for the next three years toured the royal courts of Europe giving performances.

When, at the age of three, he watched his sister having keyboard lessons and reached up to press the keys of the clavier, it was certainly not his first experience of musical instruments. His father taught him minuets "in his fourth year" and his sister says, "He could play faultlessly and with the greatest delicacy, and keeping exactly in time."

It is not absolutely impossible that a being can be relatively new. But if the trail of footprints peters out only a few hundred yards down the beach, look carefully. Before that, there may be slitherings of something that passed this way on its belly. Or wing prints in the subtleties of the air. But the majority of us have long provenances; time tracks that stretch back endlessly.

They can be accessed.

This is not to say that everyone can do it or that it is easy. But it *is* possible, using the Centre. And this is one method.

37. BLOWING THE FUSE

Electrical appliances are protected from sudden surges of power through the mains by a fuse. If the fuse is defective, the appliance is destroyed.

You, the appliance, are protected from a sudden surge of power through the Centre by your merit and your virtue. If this is insufficient and you persist in drawing on the Centre's power, the appliance is destroyed.

This accounts for all the great disasters that affect mankind:

- Man's inhumanity to man and other living beings (wars, genocide, slavery, sexual and economic exploitation, killing, vivisection, torture);
- Man's reckless abuse of himself (drunkenness, drug addiction, lying, stealing).

Everything you do is done with the spiritual power which emanates from the Centre. The Centre is the source and origin of all its offshoots. It is their very being. Serious misuse of the Centre or any of its parts results in the blowing of the fuse. Madness. Followed by a spiralling down into those lower planes of suffering which you can preview for yourself if you have learned how to use the Centre. (See page 57).

Replacing the fuse means reinstating Ethics.

Basic ethics is:

Cease from all evil. Do what is good. Cleanse one's mind.

Where "*evil*" is broadly defined as doing to others what you would not welcome others doing to you. And "*cleansing the mind*" means removing all negative states of mind and negative impulses towards others.

EPILOGUE

A great deal has been written about the centres. Usually they are called *chakras*. This is a Sanskrit word which means wheel or disc. A Sanskrit word is used because much of the research has been done, or at least written about, in India.

Books that contain information about the chakras have not necessarily been written by authors who have actually experienced all or any of what they write about. Often they write about what they have read in other books. These other books may have been written by authors who found the information in still *other* books, which may have been written by authors.... This is the literary version of Chinese Whispers.

Somebody, sometime, probably, experienced something. Certainly, many somebodies have exercised the imaginations of those who read their books and have perhaps given them pleasure.

Giving pleasure to people by writing is not to be derided. People read to be entertained and it is by no means necessary for a book to be factual for it to entertain. Quite the reverse.

Not all those who enjoy *Alice in Wonderland* believe that a ten-year-old girl really did fall down a rabbit hole into a world peopled by anthropomorphic characters, including a caterpillar three inches high that smokes a hookah and offers Alice what seems to be a kind of magic mushroom.

There are books whose main claim to our attention is not that they entertain but that they are true. Quite rightly, we often avoid this kind of book because we don't *want* too much truth to put a dampener on our enjoyment of life. We don't want to read about the horrors of factory farming or the force-feeding of geese to produce pâté de foie gras or the conditions in which coalminers and sewage workers have to work to earn a living.

We will (may) put up with the truth if it makes us live a little longer (health tips or horror stories about lung cancer) or makes us more attractive to women (how to get rid of head lice and B.O.).

However, there is a kind of truth that appears occasionally in print about things that we ought to know because they directly affect our well-being and long-term happiness.

This is such a book.

But this book contains details of things that we may not have experienced. Like all those books about "chakras" – invisible wheels spinning around in key areas of our bodies.

How do we know whether to believe any of it?

Well we don't, so we shouldn't. We shouldn't believe things which don't correspond to our own experience. Not important things anyway.

We need not *disbelieve* them. We should suspend judgement until we have experienced them for ourselves.

Take unicorns. Unicorns caused a bit of a stir in the Middle Ages. They had been mentioned in the Bible but had always proved elusive. Invariably, when they were seen it was somewhere else (such as India). And by someone else.

This did not deter artists in the Middle Ages painting them with considerable consistency. In Europe, the definitive image became a rather elegant, usually white horse with a horn growing straight out of the centre of its forehead.

They fascinated those people in the Middle Ages who had the means and the leisure to be fascinated by such things and had never actually seen one. These were a minority. They did not fascinate the majority who were mostly fascinated by how to find their next meal and live until tomorrow and avoid the Plague and conscription and the stocks and a good flogging.

The image became standard. Those who organised fayres and entertainments, seeing that there was money in it, fitted fake horns to the heads of docile horses and exhibited them along with Bearded Women, Fire Eaters, Bear Baiters, Cornish Wrestlers and other forerunners of modern Association Football.

And people *believed* it. Even those who, when they were not attending fayres, spent their time trying to find their next meal or living until tomorrow, rather than poring over illuminated manuscripts at pictures of horses with barbers' poles stuck on their noses.

Yet, indeed, someone had originally seen something, somewhere, sometime.

Anyone who has ever had any experience of horses and rhinoceroses will be keenly aware of important differences between them. This is where experiencing something for yourself comes in.

It is not unpleasant to stroll through an English meadow, where horses are grazing, collecting buttercups. (*You* are collecting the buttercups, not the horses.)

If while you were doing this you were to encounter a rhinoceros, you would notice three things. One, it looks very little like a horse. Two, it has already killed all the real horses using a particularly vicious bone structure at the front of its head. Three, unlike any real horse, it will charge the farmer's Land Rover in which you have taken refuge, whether it is moving or not, and try to demolish it.

The unicorn whose picture you admired when you were a medieval courtier is one thing. The rhino chasing your safari Land Rover is your *experience.*

So it is with this book. The first eight chapters are simple statements of the Truth. Some will recognise this immediately (where has this been all my life?). Others will reach for something else to read.

After chapter 8 it is unicorns, unicorns all the way. You may not believe it. You should not disbelieve it. You suspend judgement.

BUT, the book does provide a method, a set of instructions and a map. If you can use them, you will experience these things, or some of them. Yourself.

> *When the clouds disappear*
> *the sun is already there.*

> *When the voices stop*
> *it is already silent.*
>
> (Gnomonic Verses)

One and not two,
That's all you have to do.
One and not two.

Wherever you go,
That's all you have to know.

www.ingramcontent.com/pod-product-compliance
Lightning Source LLC
Chambersburg PA
CBHW051649040426
42446CB00009B/1047